THE LITTLE BOOK

THAT
MAKES
YOU RICH

Little Book Big Profits Series

In the *Little Book Big Profits* series, the brightest icons in the financial world write on topics that range from tried-and-true investment strategies to tomorrow's new trends. Each book offers a unique perspective on investing, allowing readers to pick and choose from the very best in investment advice today.

Books in the *Little Book Big Profits* series include:

The Little Book That Beats the Market, where Joel Greenblatt, founder and managing partner at Gotham Capital, reveals a "magic formula" that is easy to use and makes buying good companies at bargain prices automatic, enabling you to successfully beat the market and professional managers by a wide margin.

The Little Book of Value Investing, where Christopher Browne, managing director of Tweedy, Browne Company, LLC, the oldest value investing firm on Wall Street, simply and succinctly explains how value investing, one of the most effective investment strategies ever created, works, and shows you how it can be applied globally.

The Little Book of Common Sense Investing, where Vanguard Group Founder John C. Bogle shares his own time-tested philosophies, lessons, and personal anecdotes to explain why outperforming the market is an investor illusion, and how the simplest of investment strategies—indexing—can deliver the greatest return to the greatest number of investors.

The Little Book That Makes You Rich, where Louis Navellier, financial analyst and editor of investment newsletters since 1980, offers readers a fundamental understanding of how to get rich using the best in growth investing strategies. Filled with in-depth insights and practical advice, *The Little Book That Makes You Rich* outlines an effective approach to building true wealth in today's markets.

The Little Book That Builds Wealth, where Pat Dorsey, director of stock analysis for leading independent investment research provider Morningstar, Inc., guides the reader in understanding "economic moats," learning how to measure them against one another, and selecting the best companies for the very best returns. (Coming Winter 2008)

THE LITTLE BOOK

THAT
MAKES
YOU RICH

A Proven Market-Beating Formula

for Growth Investing

LOUIS NAVELLIER

FOREWORD BY STEVE FORBES

John Wiley & Sons, Inc.

Published by John Wiley & Sons, Inc., Hoboken, New Jersey.
Published simultaneously in Canada.

Wiley Bicentennial Logo: Richard J. Pacifico

For general information on our other products and services or for technical support, please contact our Customer Care Department within the United States at (800) 762-2974, outside the United States at (317) 572-3993 or fax (317) 572-4002.

Wiley also publishes its books in a variety of electronic formats. Some content that appears in print may not be available in electronic formats. For more information about Wiley products, visit our Web site at www.wiley.com.

Library of Congress Cataloging-in-Publication Data:

Navellier, Louis.
The little book that makes you rich / Louis Navellier.
    p. cm.—(Little book big profits series)
   ISBN 978-0-470-13772-7 (cloth)
    1. Stocks. 2. Investments. I. Title.
HG4661.N385 2007
332.63'22—dc22

                                                  2007024240

Printed in the United States of America.

10 9 8 7 6 5 4 3 2 1

Contents

Chapter Five
Surprise, Surprise, Surprise

Chapter Six
Sell, Sell, Sell

Chapter Seven
Expand, Expand, Expand

Chapter Eight
Let It Flow

Chapter Nine
It's All Variable

Chapter Ten
Know Your Alpha Beta

Chapter Eleven
Don't Be a Deviant

Chapter Twelve
The Zigzag Approach

Foreword

———— ≈ ————

HERE'S WHY THIS BOOK will be so helpful to you.

Most individuals in the stock market swear that they are long-term investors and that they are disciplined in their investment decisions. Alas, most end up being the exact opposite. When the market takes a hit, for instance, all too often people ask, "Is it too late to get out?" And when it comes to trading individual securities, folks are swayed by an infinite variety of factors—something they have seen on TV, heard at a cocktail party, read in a newspaper or magazine article, or spotted in a newsletter.

Result: You get whipsawed by buying too high and/or selling too low. The market masters you instead of it being the other way around.

That's why the two most pregnant phrases in investing are: "down the slope of hope" and "climbing walls of worry." In a bear market, which invariably follows a vigorous up market, people believe the downturn is an aberration. When a market rally occurs, they figure the bad news is behind them and the market is back on an upward trend. Then stocks get hit again, and this is followed by yet another so-called suckers' rally. Finally investors cry, "Just get me even and I'll never go into the market again." That's usually a stock market bottom.

Conversely, in a bull market investors are aware of the bad news and the things that can go wrong. They are cautious, wondering if the market is about to take a big hit. They either sit on their cash or go into equities very cautiously. Only in the latter stages of a bull market does euphoria take over.

Are you tired of being whipsawed by the market, of letting your emotions dominate your investing decisions, of not having a disciplined approach to fortify you in tough markets and prevent you from getting too giddy in up markets?

If so, you will enjoy—and profit from—this wee book. Louis Navellier has had a most enviable long-term investment record. Sure, he has had fallow periods, and some of his stock picks have turned out to be clunkers. But—and this "but" is key—he has a disciplined method of investing that over time has given him, and can give you, impressive, far-above-average returns.

Navellier lists eight fundamental factors that go into his stock picking (see page 3). Early on he recognized that focusing on one fundamental can lead you astray. Wall Street is one heck of an emotional place. As Louie says in this book, "The stock markets have all the psychological symptoms of your average severe schizophrenic," and "The biggest risk of all to successful growth stock investing [is] human emotions, such as fear and greed, which all too often lead us to do the wrong thing at exactly the wrong time." Wall Street is more addicted to fashions than Hollywood or the garment industry are. You don't want to fall into the rut of the flavor of the month. A particular variable may serve you well for a period of time, but it can then let you down as other investors catch on to it. The weighting Louie gives to each of his eight variables will vary over time, but he avoids the perils of focusing on only one or two that seem hot at the moment.

His book also takes great pains to discuss *reducing* risk while shooting for excellent returns. He includes an eye-opening discussion on two much talked about but sometimes misunderstood terms, beta and alpha.

Bottom line: Louie shows you how he looks for equities that can do well in whatever the overall market conditions are. And because there are always surprises lurking, he urges investors to *diversify* their portfolios—into, say, 30 to 40 equities.

So my advice is to take the time to read and ponder this little book. You will learn many useful things, and, most important, you may truly grasp the lesson that investing takes not only hard work but also stick-to-itiveness and a consistent approach. Louie Navellier demonstrates that focus and discipline will indeed fatten your portfolio with profits.

—STEVE FORBES

Preface

~

How can a little book like this claim to make you rich? That's what any skeptical reader is likely to be thinking. And if that's you, I say "Bravo!" You cannot be a successful investor if you believe every story Wall Street throws your way. But believe me, dear investor: Though I may use fun analogies, the strategy to riches I lay out page by page in this *Little Book* is no fairytale.

My name is Louis Navellier, and I'm a numbers guy, plain and simple. I've been investing in the stock market for over 27 years and within that time have helped investors beat the market nearly 4-to-1. How did I do it? I did it by investing in healthy, vital, *growing* companies.

Value investing in the manner of Warren Buffett will reward those who find the occasional undervalued company. And index investing is for those satisfied with keeping pace with the overall market (no matter how slow). But *growth investing*—finding the real power-engine companies pushing the economy forward—is what I have found to be the most potent strategy for making investors rich.

Frankly, it's what got me to where I am today. My father was a hardworking bricklayer and stonemason, so I come from humble beginnings. The wealth I've made over the years is a result of my inherited work ethic (a tireless drive I owe to my dad). That drive led me to uncover an investing formula for picking growth stocks that forever changed my life. I now live predominantly in a nice oceanfront house near Palm Beach with my beautiful wife and kids, have a number of nice cars (outside of a passion for numbers, I confess I have a real passion for cars!), and frequently utilize one of my private jets to take my colleagues and myself where we need to go when meeting with clients and folks on Wall Street.

I was one of the first in my family to go to college, and it was a proud moment for my folks to see me start at Cal State Hayward (now Cal State East Bay) in California. We all knew my years at Cal State would be life changing, but I don't think any of us knew to what extent! You see, one of my finance professors was from Wells Fargo and

I got the opportunity to work on a research project where my assignment was to build a model that mirrored the S&P 500. Yes, it was a dream assignment for a "numbers geek" like me. Putting all the quantitative calculations aside for a minute, the concept of mirroring the market sounds simple enough, right? Well, much to my surprise, the project didn't go quite as I planned. It turned out that my model did *better* than the market—a lot better! The significance was breathtaking. Back then, for years and years, I had been taught that it was impossible to beat the market. And then suddenly, I did.

I admit I was both delighted and a little bit outraged to make this discovery. I was delighted because I had unlocked a formula for finding stocks that continually outperform the market without taking on any excess risk—and outraged because I felt deceived by the very Wall Street pros I had once admired.

The day I discovered this market-beating formula, I made it my mission to help hardworking individual investors who might not have the resources that the powerful Wall Street firms do. My schedule today is hectic, but incredibly fulfilling. I write four newsletters, do regular speaking engagements around the country, and run a successful money management company in Reno, Nevada. I do it all to help empower individual investors to achieve their financial dreams. And today, in the pages of this

Little Book, I'm here to empower you with the knowledge and tools that can help make you rich.

We'll begin with my proven formula for finding growth stocks that beat the market, which combines one part powerful fundamentals—such as sales growth and cash flow (just two of the eight key variables we'll cover later on)—and two parts high quantitative marks that indicate "buy this stock now!" (as you'll soon see, this is the real moneymaker part of our formula). Best of all, this formula is also incredibly effective in flashing great big neon warning signs over the stocks you shouldn't touch with a ten-foot pole.

I've created a companion web site (www.getrichwith-growth.com) where you'll gain online access to my exclusive stock-rating database—an interactive tool that rates nearly 5,000 stocks according to my proven formula. This way, when you've finished reading this *Little Book*, you'll be able to take what you've learned cover to cover and apply it in the real world of investing, instantly!

I want this book to do what it says it will do—make you rich. I want you to be able to send your kids to college or retire in comfort or take that dream vacation you've always wanted or achieve whatever is your financial dream.

Being a successful growth stock investor allowed me to achieve my financial dreams. I hope this *Little Book* will start you on the path to doing the same.

Acknowledgments

— ≈ —

I WOULD LIKE TO THANK several people for inspiring me and encouraging me to write *The Little Book That Makes You Rich*.

First, I must thank the School of Business and Economics at California State University–Hayward (now Cal State East Bay) for providing me with a strong accounting background and exposing me to what were at the time incredibly powerful tools: Stanford University's banking simulator and Wells Fargo's mainframe computers. Using them, I was able to test, formulate, refine, and validate my quantitative and fundamental stock screening criteria. Special thanks to Professor Arnold Langsen for his inspiration and guidance, which continued long after my graduation in 1978. I would also like to acknowledge how much I appreciated Cal State Hayward's year-round curriculum, which allowed me to accelerate my education and graduate from college by the age of 20. Cal State Hayward was simply a phenomenal school that put me on the fast track to success.

Second, I have to thank all of the loyal employees and shareholders at my management company, headquartered in Reno, Nevada. I especially want to thank the dedicated management team for helping me refine my quantitative and fundamental stock-selection criteria. Together, we have expanded our system to specialize in exciting tax-efficient, trading, hedge, style-specific, and international programs. We spend every weekend researching and subsequently updating our quantitative and fundamental stock rankings on almost 5,000 stocks in order to help investors know which stocks are the best stocks on the market today. Our research never stops, and our pledge to all investors is that we will continue to uncover key stock market anomalies, both today and in the future.

Third, I must thank all of my associates at InvestorPlace Media for helping me share my knowledge and experience with thousands of individual investors through my investment newsletters. I am especially thankful and appreciative of how we have been able to provide my powerful online database to all of the subscribers. My associates at InvestorPlace Media and I are on a mission to educate, empower, and truly help investors. We are proud of our long-term performance ratings by *The Hulbert Financial Digest*, but we are prouder still of the tens of thousands of investors whom we have helped achieve their financial dreams.

Fourth, I must thank my wife, Wendy, and my children, Crystal, Chase, and Natalie, for allowing me to work extensively on weekends, when the stock market briefly stands still. I know that my passion for striving to be the best can sometimes cut into family activities, but I appreciate your support and understanding as I continue my endless quest to help investors. I certainly hope that my work ethic rubs off on my children and helps them succeed in all of their endeavors.

Finally, special thanks to Tim Melvin and Melanie Russo, who worked tirelessly on this book and to whom I am eternally grateful.

Chapter One

Let's Start at the End

At the End of the Day, It's Earnings That Matter.

IN THE CLASSIC MUSICAL, *The Sound of Music*, the character of Sister Maria (played by Julie Andrews) tells us that we should start at the beginning because "that is a very fine place to start." In our search for profits investing in growth stocks, however, we shall do the opposite of the Sister's advice and start our search at the end. The plain fact is that at the end of the day what makes for a great growth stock, one that can grow to 5, 10, or even 20 times your original investment over time, is the *fundamentals* of the company. Can the company continually sell more of its products and services at higher and higher profits? Can it continue to innovate and adapt to marketplace changes and maintain a leadership position? In the end, what makes for a great growth stock is the ability of the company to continually sell more of its goods or services at high levels of profitability.

One definitive factor I have found over the years is that change is a fact of life on Wall Street. All too often I hear a pundit or guru telling us of one *magic-bullet* variable that is most important in picking winning stocks—such as price-to-earnings ratios or price-to-cash flow. Of course, these magic-bullet fundamentals can fall out of favor quickly. The one certain thing I can tell you from all my years of investing research is that many fundamental variables have a life span, perhaps two to three years at most, before they stop working and the edge is gone. It's kind of like the great football coach Bill Walsh and his dynasty football team of the 1980s, the San Francisco 49ers. Walsh had a clear edge with his newly invented West Coast offense that befuddled teams around the league and made the Niners all but unbeatable. However, over time, teams adapted to this innovation and the edge was dulled, leading the way for new teams to develop new game plans that led to Super Bowls. The 49ers had a great run, but just like on Wall Street, once the edge is gone, the run is over. There will be periods of time that the market favors stocks with earnings momentum, and periods where operating cash flow or earnings before interest, taxes, and depreciation (EBITDA) are the darlings of the day. As soon as the dance cards are full and everyone can be found chasing after the same thing, the band will stop and the party will be over.

Because of this tendency for the game to change, I have found that it is necessary to rank stocks on more than one fundamental variable, and from time to time I may even tweak the weighting of each variable. When my team and I were building our stock selection program, we looked at hundreds of fundamental factors to determine which ones ultimately had the most influence on the performance of a company's stock price. We also examined which factors are in favor on Wall Street and driving stock prices up or down at any given time. We use this powerful model to sort through the thousands of stocks traded to find those most likely to become high-powered growth stock winners.

I have found that there are eight tried-and-true key fundamental factors that drive stellar stock price performance and have stood the test of time:

1. *Positive earnings revisions:* when Wall Street analysts indicate that business is even better than anticipated

2. *Positive earnings surprises:* announced corporate earnings that are higher than analysts expected
3. *Increasing sales growth:* continuous rapid sales growth of a company's products
4. *Expanding operating margins:* corporate profit margins that are expanding
5. *Strong cash flow:* a company's ability to generate free cash flow after expenses
6. *Earnings growth:* sustained earnings growth quarter to quarter
7. *Positive earnings momentum:* earnings that are accelerating year over year
8. *High return on equity:* high overall corporate profitability

These indicators measure the financial health of a company, how well their products are selling, and whether they are able to maintain and even increase a very high level of profitability. A company that scores very high across all eight of our *fundamental* model variables is highly likely to have all the characteristics of a potential 10-bagger growth stock that we want to add to our portfolio right away.

The first of our eight key variables is **earnings revisions**. We search for stocks whose earnings estimates are revised upward by the Wall Street analysts who cover and research these companies. After all the fallout from Tyco,

WorldCom, and Enron, along with the crusade by Eliot Spitzer, this factor is becoming more important. Analysts are so cautious that they have to be really impressed to keep raising their estimate of corporate profits. Apple is a great example. In a 90-day period in 2006, analysts who follow the stock raised their estimates multiple times.

The second fundamental variable is **earnings surprises**. This measures how far above or below the overall consensus estimates of Wall Street analysts the actual reported earnings are. Here we are looking for stocks that exceed what Wall Street believes they can achieve. Oil and energy stocks, for example, have continuously earned far more than the analysts thought they could. Since the corporate scandals and Wall Street prosecutions and investigations made by Elliot Spitzer, most analysts tend to be conservative in their estimates. Several years ago, they estimated that oil would sell for around $40 a barrel. As oil prices went to $60 and beyond, the earnings were far in excess of what was predicted and many energy stock prices skyrocketed!

Third is **sales growth**. All we do here is compare the current quarter's sales increase against the rate of increase from the same quarter for the prior year. Companies that show increasing sales at a very high rate are among the best candidates to become big winners over time. If a company can continually increase sales over long periods of time, then it would seem to indicate that they have a product or service that is very much in demand. We look for companies that show year-over-year sales increases of 20 percent or more. Most recently, sales growth led us to a company named Hansen Natural. This maker of the very popular Monster energy drink has seen sales rise from 100 million in 2003 to over 500 million in 2006, a revenue increase of over 65 percent annually.

The fourth of our eight fundamental variables is **operating margin growth**. A company's operating margin is simply the profits left after direct costs such as salary and overhead are subtracted. We then look at whether this percentage margin is contracting or growing year over year. A company's operating margin will increase when its product is in such high demand that the company can continue to raise prices for the product or service without an offsetting increase in costs. A great example of this type of margin expansion is a company named Bolt Technology. As demand for their seismic equipment used to explore for oil increased along with oil prices, profit margins went from 8 percent in 2004 to over 40 percent in 2006. This type of profitability increase was among the leading factors that (adjusted for splits) led the stock from $8 a share to over $40.

Batting fifth on our growth stock selection team is **cash flow**. Cash flow is simply the amount of cash actually earned and kept by a company after paying all expenses and is often the single best measure of corporate financial health. Companies that regularly pay out more than they bring in are likely to experience severe hardship at some point. A company can show earnings, then spend all of it and then some on necessary capital expenditures—which are included in expenses on the income statement—and actually end the year with less money than they started with. We measure how much free cash flow a company has each quarter and then compare it to the total market capitalization of the company to see what investors are willing to pay for shares at any point in time.

The next variable is **earnings growth**. This measurement finds those companies who earn more money year after year. It is usually measured in terms of earnings per share. Earnings per share (EPS) is just the company's earnings divided by the number of shares they have outstanding. Companies that are continually growing earnings year over year get a higher score than those that aren't. That's why we call it *growth investing*. Most of the stocks we buy show strong, continual year-over-year growth. For instance, DirecTV Group went from a loss of 21 cents a share in 2004 to earning well over a dollar a share in 2006. In real numbers, they went from losing $375 million to making over $1 billion. That's growth!

The seventh fundamental feature we are looking for is **earnings momentum**. This simply measures the percentage increase of earnings year over year. Companies that are accelerating and growing earnings faster year over year are stronger candidates for our portfolio than those where earnings are slowing. A great example of what we are looking for is seen in a company like Steve Madden (SHOO), where from 2004 to 2005 they grew earnings by over 61 percent. That's a great number, right? They then turned around and earned over 117 percent more the following year! This type of powerful performance drove the stock from around $10 a share to over $40 in two years.

Last but not least on our list is **return on equity**. Return on equity (ROE) is a measure of corporate profitability. It is calculated by dividing the earnings per share by the equity (book value) per share. The higher this number, the more profitable a company is and the higher return management is providing to shareholders. Companies that are dominant in their industry tend to earn very large returns on the equity invested. The search for high ROE stocks has helped us find such profit machines as International Game Technology, AES Corporation, Loews, and First Marblehead.

To give you some idea of how powerful these eight indicators are, my research staff and I went back and reviewed how stocks showing the strongest rating in each of the eight categories have performed over the past several years. We found that the highest-rated stocks in each category outperformed the universe of stocks we follow. The table below lists all eight of our variables and shows how much better in price performance they have done than all other stocks combined:

Variable	Outperformance of Universe Over Three Years
Earnings revisions	10%
Earnings surprises	13%
Sales growth	7%
Operating margin growth	61%
Free cash flow	59%
Earnings growth	30%
Earnings momentum	60%
Return on equity	30%

As you can see, some clearly have done better than others, although, because this measures outperformance, clearly all have done better than the market as a whole. But why not just use the variables that score the highest? For the same reason that the 49ers aren't in the playoffs: Just as everyone learned to run and defend the West Coast offense and it became a less powerful weapon, as soon as we relied on just a few measures, the game would change and we would miss great stocks. Instead we plug all eight variables into our model and come up with a basic overall fundamental weightings. The amount each variable counts may be changed or tweaked over time, but all eight variables are considered when searching for the big winning stocks. It is the combination of variables that has allowed us to discover such great stocks as America Movil (up 400 percent in three years), Apple (up over 300 percent in two years), and Hansen Natural (up over 1,000 percent in three years.) It also helps us to avoid stocks that are likely to become disappointing investments and to sell those that have been great winners but are starting to show signs of deteriorating fundamentals. By concentrating on the numbers, and *just* the numbers, we try to take the guesswork out of picking winning stocks. I may not be able to tell which MP3 player manufacturer, tennis shoe company, or nanotechnology venture will pan out to be a huge winner, but relying on the numbers has identified the winning stocks.

In this book I am going to show how these variables, combined with risk and portfolio management, can indeed make you rich over time. I will explain each variable in depth so you can understand just how powerful they are and how they influence stock prices. These fundamental variables are the result of a lot of research and effort by myself and my staff and have enabled me to outperform the stock market year after year in good times as well as in bad. I will also show how to use *reward/risk measurements* to determine when these fundamentally superior companies are experiencing intense buying pressure that will make the price of their stock climb steadily higher. Of course, it is not enough to know what and when to buy, so I will also show you how to determine that a stock has become too risky and that buying pressure is abating and it needs to be sold.

I will also show you how to use *portfolio management techniques* to take a lot of the day-to-day risks of investing in stocks out of the growth stock equation. I will even talk about ways to manage the biggest risk to successful growth stock investing—human emotions such as fear and greed that all too often lead us to do the wrong thing at exactly the wrong time. It is difficult to be buying amid panic, and selling when everyone else is excited about the stock market, but I am going to teach you how to use my system to do exactly that.

Speaking of my system, I will also give you a powerful tool to help you select market-beating stocks and manage your portfolio. I maintain an enormous database at my offices in Reno, Nevada. This database has all the fundamental data and daily price records for nearly 5,000 stocks. I will give you access to the database through a web site that has been set up specifically for readers of this book. There you will find a tool that rates individual companies based on each of the eight variables we'll discuss here, as well as on how much buying pressure their shares are currently experiencing in the marketplace. Once you understand from this book how powerful this system for picking growth stocks can be, you will find it an incredibly useful tool for finding the top-performing stocks on Wall Street and blending them into a successful wealth-building portfolio.

Let's get started, shall we?

Chapter Two

Counting On Growth

~

Growth Can Be Measured. Count on It.

TRADITIONAL INVESTMENT and Wall Street analysis consists of talking to company management, customers, and suppliers, and then building complex hypothetical models to try and guess future financial results. Analysts spend their days on the phone and attending meetings to try to uncover winning stock picks. This process is both ponderous and relatively unsuccessful. In its attempt to *sell the story*, all too often the Street gets caught up in the story and starts believing its projections as the gospel truth. Storytelling leads investors down a path of underperformance and losses.

Listening to stories can be great fun. It can be entertaining and interesting. A great way to spend an evening is to sit around with a few adult distilled beverages and share stories with friends. But this is a lousy way to pick stocks and can cost you a lot of money over the long run (and sometimes even the short run). Wall Street loves to find and sell stories. It is the basis of the business. In the late 1960s, the word was *conglomeratization*. Those who listened and believed lost enormous amounts of money. In the early 1980s, the story was all about oil and gas and real estate. Those who listened and believed lost enormous amounts of money. In the late 1990s, the buzz was the *paradigm shift* caused by the technology and Internet revolution. Those who listened and believed lost enormous amounts of money. The more seductive and alluring the investment story, the more likely it is that one is entering the land of financial dragons with Saint George nowhere in sight. The better the story sounds, the more you should beware.

Our ancestors believed in things we now know to be completely wrong. People seem to have a need to invent reasons for their world and what goes on in it. Humans have attributed crop failure to irate gods. Cattle were struck because someone failed to sacrifice the right animal to the troll under the mountain. We now know that crops fail due to overplanting and incompatible soil.

Cattle disappear because of real-life predators such as wolves. The reality is that, short of hard science, we invent reasons for the things that happen in the world, and this tendency to believe in the magical or otherworldly takes place every day on Wall Street. Analysts make claims such as, "The stock was going to be fine but it ran into a double ascending lateral triangle that caused it to break down," or, "The moving average dipped when it should have swerved." More fundamentally we hear things like, "Well, the patents should have been granted but the stubborn old FDA just refused to overlook those 2,000 unexplainable deaths of subjects taking the new wonder drug." Heed this: Stocks don't dip on lateral triangles or dipping moving averages and companies don't run into financial problems because of the FDA. In all cases there is a pattern that is discernable with scientific analysis.

I am a numbers guy. Numbers and stocks are two of my greatest passions in life, and fortunately I have been able to combine them into a long and successful career picking growth stocks. I believe that the proof is in the numbers and that a careful study and analysis of the numbers can help us find stocks with growth potential and big gains in the future while avoiding stories and mumbo-jumbo. Getting caught up in the story can cause investors to believe the hype surrounding a stock or a market and stay long after they should have exited. It was pure numbers-based research that led my firm to sell Cisco and Sun Microsystems in December 2000 and to begin to buy energy stocks and conservative companies, such as Loews and United Healthcare, that didn't participate in the tech bubble. Those who listened to the tech story stayed long after the party ended and had to pay the bill. It was pure *quantitative and statistical analysis* that had us buying homebuilders in 2002 just as they began their multiyear run to a constant string of new highs.

More and more, society understands that it is often the numbers and math of a situation that have the most meaning. Meaningful, real answers, as opposed to mysterious forces, come from scientific analysis of the numbers underlying a situation. Analyzing things from a subjective point of view allows us to color situations with our own opinions, hopes, and dreams and to be influenced by others. And there is just way too much information of a subjective nature floating around us every day. How do we even begin to decipher which is right and which isn't? It's impossible! Malcolm Gladwell pointed out a prime example of this in his book, *Blink,* where he told of a new, simple mathematical algorithm that helped emergency room doctors quickly and simply assess whether a patient was having a heart attack. Researchers discovered that doctors had too much information coming at them too fast, so boiling it down to a simple formula sped up the process, made diagnosis more efficient, and saved lives.

The use of statistical and quantitative analysis has also spread to the sports world. I like to talk about sports with friends and associates, but I approach it differently than most people since I am more clinical and analytical and less emotional about teams and their players. I have always said that if I was ever going to manage a basketball team I would do it by the numbers. I would rank players on all the key statistical categories and select those who ranked the highest overall. We have seen many great shooters in basketball. Allan Iverson and Pistol Pete Maravich are two who come immediately to mind. They could shoot lights out but never came close to a championship. Once Kobe Bryant was separated from Shaq's rebounding and inside scoring ability, the Lakers became average at best. Success comes from putting together a team that excels in all areas—steals, assists, rebounds, blocks, and foul shooting.

I would like to claim that I invented and developed the statistical approach to sports team management, but someone beat me to the punch. In his bestseller, *Moneyball*, Michael Lewis tells the story of Billy Beane, the general manager of the Oakland Athletics. Beane is considered something of a revolutionary among general managers and was the first to rely on the pure numbers. Sure, Bill James kept track of everything trackable about the game in his baseball encyclopedia for years, but that was for fans, not managers. Beane challenged conventional wisdom and used the numbers, and pretty much *just* the numbers, to assemble his team. This was a major affront to those who believed that you had to have an eye for talent (a story, if you will). Numbers couldn't put together winning teams; only experts could. Beane developed formulas to measure a player's statistics against the cost of the player's contracts. Using the numbers, Beane has turned the Athletics into one of the winningest teams in baseball with a fraction of the payroll cost of the Yankees or Red Sox. The A's are also wildly profitable and they share a market with the San Francisco Giants. In fact, both teams have subsequently hired baseball quantitative analysts to help manage their rosters.

The use of statistical and quantitative analysis continues to grow. One recent, fascinating television show is *Numbers*, a one-hour drama about a math genius who uses mathematical models and statistics to solve crime problems for the FBI. This type of analysis is widely used by law enforcement to crack cases, by insurance companies to assign rates to different drivers in different locations, and even by casinos to separate gamblers from their hard-earned money. In fact, one of the most popular games today is poker, a game where many of the top players are quant folks and rely on numbers to win. So, if statistical and quantitative thinking works in so many areas of life, why wouldn't it work in the stock market? The fact is that it does.

One of the more important aspects about using the numbers and just the numbers is that it keeps us from falling in love with a story. Because of our reliance on just the numbers, both fundamental and quantitative, we are one of the few firms that can claim to have made a substantial amount of money in Enron. Everyone now knows the Enron story and the accounting and trading frauds that took the company all the way into bankruptcy. What they forget is that Enron was once a powerful growth company with rapidly rising sales and earnings. We were in the stock while it was in a growth mode but exited long before the headlines hit, because the numbers showed weakening fundamentals and increased risk. We didn't know the backstory, but the numbers alerted us to problems before the newspapers reported the bad news.

Numerical reliance saved us in Tenet Healthcare, as well. In the late 1990s into 2001, Tenet was a powerful growth story. They run a chain of hospitals and their business in the United States and Europe was growing at a rapid clip. Then, in late 2002 and the early months of 2003, came allegations of impropriety, overcharging Medicare, and bribing doctors to use their facilities. Some Tenet doctors in Redding, California were doing unnecessary heart surgeries! The SEC began looking into their billing practices and public disclosures. Long before this happened, we exited the stock when the fundamentals declined and volatility increased in November 2002. From 2001 to today, the stock has fallen from the mid-50s to just $7.50 a share!

Relying on just the numbers has helped us find growth stocks before Wall Street turned them into stories, and it has helped us exit before the story ended. Wall Street sells stories. I trust numbers. I can't always trust the Wall Street sales machine. But I can trust the numbers from my database. Count on it.

Chapter Three

Emotional Rescue

~

The Market Doesn't Care How You Feel about a Stock.

IN THEIR HIT SONG, "Emotional Rescue," the Rolling Stones promised to come to the emotional rescue of a poor unloved girl. Much as the Stones can save the broken heart of the lovelorn, numbers can rescue investors. I have learned some valuable things about numbers over the years. One of the chief things I have learned is that numbers do not have emotions. They don't panic; they don't get greedy. They don't have an argument with their spouse or associates and make bad decisions as a result.

They don't have one too many at happy hour and make bad choices the next morning from cloudy thinking. They don't care about Uncle Fred's stock pick or that the cousin of the guy down the street has made millions in an Internet cancer-curing mutual fund. Humans are affected by so many things each and every day of their lives. It is part of being human. Some people may be better than others at keeping their emotions at bay, but no one is a robot.

Although it may make me a bit of a geek, when it comes to the stock market I find that relying only on the input from the numbers keeps me from making the type of emotional decisions that humans are hardwired to make. There is a school of thought and research that follows the emotional mistakes investors make, called *behavioral finance*. Before we get into the numbers, what they mean, and how to put them to use, I want to take some time to review some of the common human errors found in investing so that you can avoid them in your own decision-making process. You may become a bit geekier about your investing process, but you'll also get richer.

One of the worst and most common emotional mistakes is referred to as *gambler's fallacy*. There is a tendency among people to think that when a coin has been tossed five times and it lands on heads all five times it is much more likely to land on tails the next time. This is totally incorrect. The odds of it being tails are exactly what they were the first five times:

fifty-fifty. Each flip occurs separately and independently of the others. It *doesn't have to* land on tails. And just because the market has been up or down the past several days doesn't necessarily mean it has to do anything one way or the other. Day to day, the market can be quite random, and the day's prices will likely be influenced by that particular day's events, not what has happened over recent trading sessions. In spite of this, I constantly hear investors say things like, "It can't go down any more." Well, guess what—it can, and it will take your money with it as it does.

Although I have been a part-time Nevada resident for the last 20 years (my offices are located in Reno), it may surprise you to learn that I do not gamble. As a numbers person, I know the odds and would rather not waste my time. Although I know how to "count cards" for blackjack and stack the odds in my favor, the practice is illegal in Nevada and I have no desire to get on a casino backlist even though I rarely set foot in casinos. The International Game Technology (IGT) folks in Reno that manufacture all the gaming equipment are experts in building machines that lure gamblers with bright colors, enticing sounds, and continuously rising progressive jackpots via their networked machines. The IGT folks are experts in *conditioning* humans, just like the famous psychologist, B.F. Skinner, who was an expert in conditioning pigeons and rats. The stock market is not so dissimilar to the casinos and also likes to condition humans.

One of the worst tendencies of investors is to sell winners far too soon and hold on to losing stocks. The old saying, that you can't go broke taking a profit, has killed more investor portfolios than Attila the Hun did Romans. If you take small 5 percent to 10 percent profits on your winners but continually take huge losses on your losers, holding onto the belief that it will come back, your overall results will look pretty bleak. Look at it this way: The best stock pickers in the history of the market might be right about 70 percent of the time. (I doubt that they are right that much, but let's use the high number for the sake of argument.) Let's say you have a $100,000 stock portfolio. If you take 5 percent profits on your winners, that is $3,500 gain. If you hold your losers too long and lose an average of 20 percent, that's a $6,000 loss. The end result is that you are picking the best stocks but losing money every year! Now, let's reverse this. Say you picked 30 percent winning stocks and made 50 percent on them each year. That is a $15,000 profit. If you limit your loss to 5 percent on losing picks, you would lose $3,500. The net result is an overall profit of $11,500! These examples are extreme but make the point that by selling the bad picks and keeping the good ones you will prevent yourself from transforming your profits into portfolio poverty.

The flip side to selling winners too soon is just as dangerous. I call it "falling in love." Because we focus on owning a widely diversified portfolio of stocks with powerful fundamentals and pass our risk/reward tests, we will, from time to time, hold stocks that become huge winners. Over many months or even multiple years, it is not unusual for us to have stocks in our portfolios that have appreciated 100 percent, 200 percent, and even 300 percent from the time of original purchase. But, as Ecclesiastes reminds us, there is a time for everything, including a time to sell. When the fundamentals begin to break down or the stock becomes too risky based on my analysis, it is simply time to get out. But investors who have experienced a great ride on a stock are sometimes reluctant to sell.

We posted some huge returns in various energy-related stocks, but as the fundamental and quantitative grades of these stocks decayed, we systematically sold these stocks. We started moving out of oil and other energy-related stocks in late 2005 and 2006, as they became too risky. By 2007, it was clear that we were right to sell, due to increasingly erratic earnings and rising volatility. However, some investors and subscribers told me that they did not want to sell, that oil is going up forever, that they don't want to pay taxes, that it is their favorite stock. These objections mark all the usual symptoms of falling in love with a stock. You can show love to stocks, but stocks can't love you back. When they become too risky, you simply have to sell them and move on, even if they have made you rich. Fortunately, the web site I set up for readers of this book (www.getrichwithgrowth.com) will make selling easy, since you can sort your stocks in order of attractiveness and prioritize what stocks to sell. Too many investors become like deer caught in headlights and freeze when they review their stock portfolios. Selecting great stocks is only half the battle. You need to act when it's time to sell to take the profit and move on to even better stocks or cut losses to avoid dangerous pain.

Figure 3.1, showing eBay stock performance from 2003 to 2005, illustrates the point. We began buying eBay in March 2003 as the company was beating analyst estimates and having estimates raised almost daily. We had a wonderful ride in the stock, but eventually the stock became too volatile and risky to continue to hold, and I advised my newsletter readers that it was time to sell. Just as with oil and other energy-related stocks in 2006, we saw some succumb to the familiar falling-in-love symptoms, and these folks held tight. As you can see, these investors may have loved eBay, but it didn't love them back. By August 2006, it had fallen back to the original purchase price. Investing should not be a roundtrip proposition. You don't want to experience riding a stock to a huge gain only to hold it while it falls back in price. The experience will be a painful lesson in the value of focusing on the cold numbers.

FIGURE 3.1   eBay's Lifecycle, 2003–2005

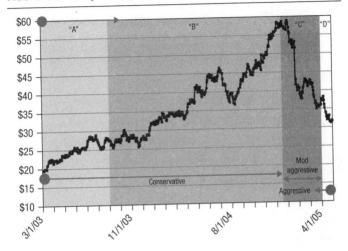

Another powerful emotional and mental mistake is what is frequently referred to by behavioral scientists as *hindsight theory*. When we look back over history, we tell ourselves that we knew something was going to happen before it did. The Internet bubble that burst in 2001 is a powerful example. Everyone now claims that they saw it coming. They just knew that the market had reached unsustainable highs and that the bubble would burst and take all the high-risk investors and day traders to the cleaners. So if everyone knew in advance, then how come they lost all that money? Almost no one admits that they hung around for the whole ride and lost money in the meltdown, yet millions of people lost billions of dollars in that time frame. Most *did not* see it coming, but the numbers *did*. As technology stocks became overly volatile and increased in risk, we were selling them and buying larger more stable companies and moving into energy stocks based on our fundamental and quantitative factors.

Investors also tend to fall victim to what Warren Buffett likes to call the *rearview-mirror effect*. We tend to be the most influenced by what has happened recently instead of what is happening right now. As the market goes higher, individuals (and institutions—after all, mutual funds and hedge funds are run by humans) tend to become more and more bullish; when the market has sold off for an extended period, they become more and more reluctant to buy. We see this behavior in trading tendencies of the market all the time. Through 1987, the single-highest-volume month in the history of the NYSE was August 1987, the exact month the market peaked. We saw it again in 2000, with volume peaking in September 2000 and then falling off over the next few years of relentless selling pressure. In fact, after the sell-off, volume was less than half what it was at the market high. As we saw with the coin-toss example, the market is forward looking. Relying on hindsight can have devastating results. In 2002, as investors were panicked, scared, and underinvested, we focused on what the numbers and our quantitative research told us, and we bought. In 2003, after the statue fell in Baghdad, dramatically lower interest rates, and pending dividend tax relief, investors finally shook off their fears and moved aggressively into stocks we had already selected based on the numbers.

We can't help our emotional and mental biases. Some are hardwired into us from birth. Some, such as the herd instinct, where we follow what everyone else is doing, are just part of the social environment in which we live. It is much easier to take the pain of market losses when everyone else is being battered, too. This herd instinct protects us from admitting that the mistake was ours and ours alone.

We also have a tendency to think that we are above average, just a little smarter than everyone else. It has been well documented by several studies that over 80 percent of all students taking a class think that they will be in the top 50 percent of students. In the world of money, if you ask fund managers, namely those who are not index fund managers, if they can outperform the market, they will pretty much answer "yes." In spite of their claims to greatness, we know that less than half of them will outperform the market in any given year, much less over an extended period of time.

We also like to have our opinions confirmed by others, especially so-called experts. Because of this, we will search and find information, data, and analysis that will confirm our opinion. If you want to see this bias in action magnified, talk to someone who is bearish on stock prices. They will cite chapter and verse of all the doom and gloom columnists who share their opinion and drag out charts, graphs, and slide shows that clearly demonstrate how and why the world is going to end. They have their opinion, and it's confirmed by others. Any evidence to the contrary will be ignored!

We also have a tendency to congratulate ourselves for our brilliance when we succeed, but blame outside influences for our failures. When a stock we picked goes up, it is because we are clever and made the right choice. When a stock we picked goes down, it's the economy, the Federal Reserve, the stupid broker, or those gosh-darned hedge funds that made things go wrong. We could not have possibly made such a bad choice. In my office, we refer to this as confusing a "bull market for brains." A potentially fatal side effect of this all-too-human trait is what happens when we get good results from bad decisions: We do the same thing again, usually to bad outcome. Not only do we lose money; we lose the time we might have spent making improvements in our portfolio.

I have a friend who trades options, who once remarked that the worst thing that can happen to a novice, unknowledgeable options trader is to make money on his first trade. This leads him to believe he actually knows what he is doing, and losses are sure to follow in large numbers. Just because a losing strategy made money one time does not mean it will next time, especially if the first time was the result of random luck and not good decision making.

All of these characteristics and biases are part of being human. When put into play in the stock market, they can lead to serious loss and damage to your net worth. I have not figured out how to stop being human, and I do not think you will be able to, either. I know that I can be a sucker for a great story, or get lulled into a false sense of security, or believe my own hype, or even follow the herd, which is why I steer clear of it all when it comes to making money in stocks and instead stick with the numbers.

Chapter Four

Revise, Revise, Revise

~

*Changing Minds Leads to
Changing Prices.*

LET'S TAKE A CLOSER look at the eight fundamentals I mentioned earlier. They are the characteristics that have proven to be the hallmark of great growth stocks over my years in this business. The first of our eight is **earnings revisions**.

Working as a Wall Street analyst is a pretty good job. You get to travel around to visit companies, talk with corporate executives, write reports, and talk to big investors. The job pays pretty well, too. Actually, it pays *really* well. I know there can be long hours and some stress, but working in a nice office and having an apartment in mid-town Manhattan is not exactly being an itinerant ditch digger, is it? In fact, it is such a good job that if I had a job as a Wall Street analyst one of my first concerns every day would be to make sure I didn't screw up badly enough to get myself fired. I have long held that not getting fired is the top priority of every analyst.

The best way not to lose this good job is to not be wrong. The quarterly earnings estimates that analysts produce are among the most closely watched numbers on Wall Street and around the world, and those analysts who most accurately guess the numbers are well rewarded with large bonuses and selection to the All-Star analyst list put out annually by *Institutional Investor* magazine. Being named to this list is a career maker and usually leads to a nice raise as well. But let's be honest. Analysts issue *estimates*—educated guesses, to be sure, but guesses none-theless. Even the best analyst will be wrong from time to time. As we already noted, if analysts guess too high and the company reports lower earnings than the guessti-mate, there's a good chance that the price of the compa-ny's shares will fall. If, however, analysts guess too low and the company earns *more* than expected, it's taken as good news and very often the stock spikes higher. The moral here is that if you are going to be wrong anyway, be too low rather than too high. Nobody is going to lose their job if the guess is on the low side and the stock goes up in price on the "error." Be too high too many times, and it's likely you'll be banished from the industry and hoping to get a job at any accounting firm instead of living the good life in midtown Manhattan. For this very self-serving reason, analysts do not like to raise their estimates of earnings unless there is very compelling evidence that business is much better than expected. Because of the potential job loss due to too-high analyst estimates, analysts raising their estimates on a company is an incredibly bullish sign of very bright times ahead for the stock.

To be fair to analysts, there are reasons for them to be conservative in their estimates beyond self-preservation. Since the Internet bubble burst of 2001, several regulatory and legal factors have come into play that impact analyst estimates. First is Regulation FD (fair disclosure). This regulation was passed to prevent one analyst or investor from having access to information about a company that wasn't available to everyone else. Rather than open the vault of corporate secrets to everyone equally instead of a few select favorites, companies have become even more tight-lipped and release less information than before the SEC passed these rules. In possession of less information than before, analyst estimates are far less accurate in a post–Regulation FD world. Analysts know that they have less information and are therefore reluctant to raise estimates without incredibly strong information. The Sarbanes-Oxley Act of 2002 has also had an impact. It made the way companies account for and disseminate information much more regulated and restricted and set stiff penalties for violations. This further reduces the flow of information to Wall Street. Again, in the face of restricted information, an analyst has to be wildly enthusiastic to raise his estimate of the next earnings report. No longer can he wine, dine, and woo friends inside the company to give him advance notice of pending good news. What used to be accepted practice can now lead to a visit to a nice cozy federal prison cell.

Thus, analysts now tend to be slow to raise their estimates each quarter. Guess too high, and the stock will drop and you lose your job; guess too low, and the stock rises and no one cares that you were wrong. When an estimate is raised, it has tremendous positive implications for a company and its stock. Stocks, as we have discussed, are priced on their earnings and the expectation for those earnings. If the expectation is up, then the stock should be worth more and rise in price to reflect that fact. Not only does upward revision mean good news in the short term; it has positive implications looking further out, as well. Remember that, above all, analysts don't want their estimates to be too high. So, rather than be too high and set up the potential for the stock to go down, if you think the company will earn another 25 cents a share next quarter, why not allow a little breathing room for yourself by raising your estimate only 15 cents or so? No point sticking your neck out and being wrong on the upside too often.

The second reason that upward earnings revisions have a long-term positive effect is that business has a certain cyclicality to it. Once things begin to catch fire and sales and earnings move at a fast clip, they tend to do so for a while. The combination of these two factors is the biggest reason that once an analyst issues an upward earnings projection it is very likely that more are on the way.

Once the estimate has been raised, all the institutional investors at mutual funds and hedge funds begin to react to the news. In the old days before Reg FD, the ones who generated the biggest commission dollars got the first call and could begin to accumulate stock ahead of the pack, but those days are gone. All the buy-side players have models they use to value stocks. Once they plug in the new number, the stock will appear to be worth more in their models and they will rush in to buy while it's still cheap. Because the amount of money available in these funds is enormous, it takes several days for them to accumulate their position, and as they do so they push up the price. The rising price often brings in other buyers, such as the momentum types who like to buy stocks hitting new highs and surf along the wave of rising prices.

There are a couple of potential pitfalls to earnings revisions. One is accounting fraud. It is not as prevalent as it was in the late 1990s, but it still exists. Companies release information to the analysts in a managed fashion so that business looks better than it is. We will examine this in greater detail later, but it does happen and causes some analysts to raise guidance when in fact business is not that good. Another pitfall can be seen in companies that are in a commodity-type business that experiences rising earnings due solely to higher commodity prices. As quickly as some prices go up, they can go back down, causing estimates to fall even faster than they rose. This is one of the reasons we use eight different factors in our stock-picking model. When earnings are managed or increases are commodity based, other factors will paint a clearer picture. Some investors and money managers trade solely on earnings revisions, but I prefer to reduce my risks by having companies where everything else is great *and* the estimates are being raised.

We have seen the power of analyst upward revisions in action over the last few years in some of the oil stocks that we held. Virtually every analyst in the world, staying true to their conservative nature, used $30/barrel oil in their pricing models coming into 2005. We came into the year locked and loaded, owning a powerful group of oil and oil services stocks. As oil prices went to $40 and then $50 a barrel and up to $70 a barrel, analysts were scrambling to play catch-up. For a while, it seemed like they were raising their guesstimates every day. We had stocks like Imperial Oil, Conoco Phillips, Suncor, and Valero in our portfolios. Valero and Suncor doubled for us from our original purchase price.

One of my favorite growth stocks in early 2007 is DirecTV. This company has done an incredible job of packaging high-definition programming and has pretty much a monopoly on some sports programming packages. Analysts have constantly underestimated viewer desire for unlimited choices for their home viewing and are playing catch-up with their projections. In late 2006, analyst estimates were raised twice in just 90 days, helping to fuel a powerful 30-percent-plus rise in this stock.

Analyst revisions have been a part of our models pretty much from the beginning and continue to be one of the more important and powerful parts of my system today. They're easily one of the best tools for picking the type of growth stocks that allow us to revise upward our estimate of our net worth and financial well-being.

Chapter Five

Surprise, Surprise, Surprise

~

*The Unexpected Can Be
Quite Profitable.*

OUR SECOND KEY VARIABLE is **earnings surprises**. Stocks with positive earnings surprises are the superstars of the growth stock world. Much like a Tom Brady who comes out of the sixth round of the NFL draft and goes on to not only win three Super Bowls but be the MVP of two, or a Tony Romo coming off the bench as a walk-on to lead the Dallas Cowboys back to the playoffs in 2006, these stocks exceed the expectations of the Wall Street analysts who follow them and experience a quick rise in status. Those that continue to exceed for several successive quarterly earnings periods often go on to become growth stock megastars. Those that disappoint and earn less than expected are better compared to Ryan Leaf, Team USA basketball in the 2004 Olympic games, or Bode Miller in the 2006 Olympic winter games. After failing to meet great expectations, they tumbled from sight and were not seen again.

What makes earnings surprises so powerful is that growth stocks are priced on investor expectations of future earnings. Analyst estimates of what a company is expected to earn each and every quarter and usually for several years into the future are published by investment brokerages, independent firms, and investment banks. Analysts carefully study the company and attempt to estimate how business and economic conditions will affect them going forward and ascertain just how much money the company will generate. Although analysts study the situation carefully and use complex models and formulas to make their predictions, it is impossible for them to know exactly what is happening within the corporate walls. When a company does exceed estimates, or falls short, the models have to be adjusted accordingly for future quarters and years. This leads to a change in investor expectations, which is how growth stocks are priced, so the price rises or falls accordingly.

Analyst estimates miss the mark for several different reasons. First, forecasting earnings to the penny each quarter is very difficult. How, for instance, could one have ever been able to predict that Hansen Natural's Monster energy drink would emerge from the very overcrowded field of caffeine- and vitamin-laced cans of liquid fuel to drive earnings up further and faster than predicted, or that Apple's iPod would emerge from the field of personal audio/video devices to create a virtual monopoly and gigantic source of profits? Another key reason that so many analysts collectively miss the mark is the herd mentality of the investment world. If we hold that many analysts have as their first objective not to make successful predictions that lead to profitable investments, but to *not get fired*, then the estimates will be within a like range and tend, mostly, to the lower side. When you have spent all the time and money needed to obtain the Ivy League MBA and get yourself a good-paying job on Wall Street, you don't want to lose that job!

The end results seems to be an environment where it is okay to be wrong, provided everyone else is wrong, too. For example, if you are the analyst at ABC brokerage, following the Acme Roadrunner and Explosives Corporation (AREC), it makes sense to call your classmate down the street at the venerable firm of Dewey, Cheatem, and Howe and get a sense of what she thinks earnings for the quarter will be. If she thinks that AREC will make a dollar per share for the quarter, it makes sense to be close to her number.

If you are a little more positive about the marketplace for deep-fried roadrunner and personal explosive devices, you might issue an estimate of $1.01; if you are a little more negative, perhaps your number will come in at $.99 a share. Most financial newspapers and web sites that follow earnings estimates show the number of analysts following a particular stock, and the high, low, and average or consensus number. It is almost amazing to see how close to each other these numbers are. Herd mentality forces analysts to follow each other and stay close to each other's estimates.

Positive earnings surprises have become more and more important in recent years. During the late-1990s Internet and technology boom, analysts were accused of, and in some cases even prosecuted by the Securities and Exchange Commission or Elliot Spitzer and his brigade of marauding Assistant District attorneys for, being too optimistic and inflating estimates of tech-company earnings. Often, in addition to the published earnings forecasts, another number floated around the Street and on some investing web sites, called the *whisper number*. This number was usually higher than the published estimates and was often said to reflect what the analyst really thought. Not only did a company have to beat the estimate, but, to truly surprise, it had to beat the whisper number, too. When a company beat both numbers, its stock price often soared. These numbers were usually available to large clients and institutions and they traded on them heavily.

Whisper numbers came to an end with the passage of the Sarbanes-Oxley Act as well as a few high-profile accusations against well-known and powerful Wall Street analysts. Sarbanes-Oxley, in particular, spelled out how analysts and companies must reveal information to the public and how the reports should be presented and disseminated. Post–Sarbanes-Oxley, an analyst who circulates a whisper number to his better clients faces prosecution, loss of job, and heavy fines. Sarbanes-Oxley has also had the effect of making companies reluctant to release information to analysts. Thus, accurate forecasting is made even more difficult. One of the results of this is that analysts tend to be much more conservative in their estimates of earnings and very reluctant to go out on a limb and raise estimates in the face of limited information.

Earnings surprises tend to persist. That is, once there is a surprise, more tend to follow, as analysts are slow to raise estimates to reflect the new reality. Stocks that surprise one quarter are likely to surprise the next quarter as well. The Figure 5.1 graph of Apple's stock in 2006 clearly shows the impact of earnings surprises over multiple quarters.

FIGURE 5.1   Apple's Positive Earnings Surprises

Data Source: Prices/Exshare

As we can see in the figure, after the original positive earnings surprise in July 2006, Apple once again surprised to the upside in October, as iPod sales remained brisk and new computers were introduced to favorable reviews.

To see the effect carried out over a multiyear period, look at Figure 5.2. Hansen Natural rose more than 400 percent over a relatively short period of time as quarter after quarter it surpassed the expectations of analysts. Starting in March 2005, they had positive earnings surprises three quarters in a row, powering the stock ever higher.

FIGURE 5.2   Hansen's Positive Earnings Surprises

Data Source: Prices/Exshare

Earning surprises can also be what stops a declining stock or lifts one that has been drifting sideways for a period of time. Through the first half of 2006, shares of Ceradyne, a maker of ceramic materials for consumer and defense applications that stand up to extreme temperatures and are corrosion resistant, had fallen from around $60 a share down to the $40 a share range and drifted pretty much down to nowhere. The earnings surprise in October lifted the shares back above the $60 level. Akami Technologies, an Internet service company whose applications help increase the speed and reliability of Internet sites, showed this same phenomenon in action. Akami basically moved sideways the first half of 2006 until it exceeded estimates for the June quarter. This was a particularly strong event as 14 different analysts followed this stock and there was less than two cents' difference in the expectations for the quarters. When they exceeded the estimates, the stock made a dramatic run from the mid-20s to over $50 a share by the end of the year!

Earnings surprise is one of the strongest factors in our fundamental rankings. Stocks that continually exceed expectations have the potential to be the Tom Bradys of the stock market and give us championship performance. Investment analysts are highly paid to make forecasts of how a company is doing. When our stocks continue to surpass those expectations, the price of the stock should continue growing to match the new, much higher forecasts and valuations.

Chapter Six

Sell, Sell, Sell

~

To Get Growth, First Someone
Has to Sell Something.

THE THIRD VARIABLE IS SIMPLY **sales growth**. One of the most important factors for a growth stock is that it is actually growing. This may sound silly, but after some of the accounting and earnings management scandals over the past six years the comment becomes somewhat less silly. The surest and truest way to measure real growth is to identify whether the company is selling more—and how much more—this year over the prior year. Dollars can be maneuvered around the income statement to massage earnings, but it is very difficult to massage top-line revenue. Sales growth is a very important part of our stock-picking model and we look for huge revenue increases.

We regularly test and track each of the variables that we use in our stock-picking model, and continually find that sales growth is one of the most powerful variables in our model. We have found that without rapid quarter-over-quarter and year-over-year sales growth it is almost impossible for a company to achieve the type of results we seek. Look at Figure 6.1 to see just how much better companies with high rates of sales growth do than those with less-spectacular revenue increases.

FIGURE 6.1   Higher-Sales-Growth Stocks Produce Higher Returns

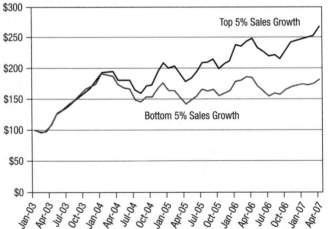

There are basically two ways for a company to achieve faster growth. The first way is for a company to have a product or service that is simply so popular and in demand that more of it will sell each and every quarter. This was the case in some of our biggest winners over the years, with companies like Chicago Mercantile Exchange and Precision Castparts. In the case of Chicago Mercantile Exchange, one of the leading futures exchanges, sales went from around 500 million to over a billion in just three short years as the markets in currency and equities boomed. Precision Castparts had sales almost triple over two years as demand for the high-tech metals used in aircraft engines exploded from pent-up demand in the airline industry. It is this type of incredible growth that fueled spectacular price rises over the same time frame. Any time a company is growing sales by 50 percent and 100 percent a year, good things are likely to happen to the stock price. First Marblehead is another great example of what happens when demand for a product takes off. As education costs have continued to increase, First Marblehead has been able to make loans and sell them off for the cash to help even more people finance their higher education. As you can see in Figure 6.2, as First Marblehead's sales exploded, so did their stock price, up 270 percent from 2004 to 2006.

The second leading cause of rapid sales growth arises in companies where the supply/demand imbalance creates

FIGURE 6.2   First Marblehead's Sales Growth

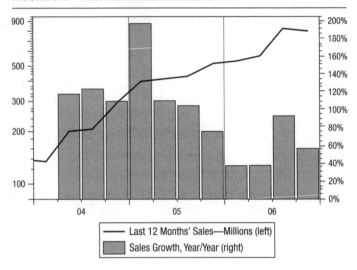

steady price increases. In other words, prices and demand rise but the costs of doing business do not go up that much. It was rapidly rising energy costs that allowed Conoco Phillips revenues to grow from $90 billion to over $185 billion in less than three years. That type of rapid revenue increase propelled the shares from $25 in 2003 to over $70 in just three years. Imperial Oil, the company that still sells under the old Esso brand in the United States, saw its sales go from $10 billion to over $24 billion in the same time frame. The stock did even better growing from $8 a share to $38 by the end of 2006.

Although I am very much a bottom-up stock picker, I often find that increased demand for a particular product or service may lead many companies in the same industry to show up in our buy lists. In other words, the entire industry group benefits from strong sales growth. When money began flowing from the stock market into banks after the Internet meltdown, the banks had to do something with all that lovely cash. They did what banks do: They made loans. All that available money began to flow into real estate as a huge cash supply and low interest rates made it possible for a lot of people to buy their first (or second) home. All these new buyers made for a real estate boom. This situation created huge revenue growth for companies like Lennar Corporation, the home builder, and Countrywide Financial, the home mortgage lender. Both stocks more than doubled in value as money moved into the real estate market from 2003 to 2005!

Accelerating revenues have been a hallmark of just about every tremendous winner I have had in my career. Companies that show lasting growth in sales are going to produce returns that are not dependent on the overall market or economy. They are in their own little world of price appreciation, which is exactly what we seek.

Slowing sales growth is one of the fastest ways to get kicked out of our portfolio. There are times when even great companies are going to find it difficult to sustain sales growth. They may even succeed themselves out of success. Intel and Microsoft are great examples of being undone by success. Both companies were once very-fast-growing businesses that absolutely revolutionized the world of computers and made vast computing power available to individuals on an unprecedented scale. However, they grew to so completely dominate their industry that there are literally very few people and businesses left to buy their products. *Everybody* has Windows and Intel Inside. Both firms now have to grow sales through product upgrades and add-ons and will likely never again see the type of sizzling prosperity they once enjoyed. We watch very carefully for declining sales growth. Because it is such a strong variable in our stock-picking success, slowing sales is a real danger sign for me.

Chapter Seven

Expand, Expand, Expand

〜

Unlike Waistlines, Expanding Margins Are Good for You.

WITH THIS VARIABLE, we're now midway through our list of eight. Our fourth variable is **operating margin expansion**. I like them fat (profit margins, that is). I focus on operating margins, which is a company's operating income divided by net sales, a figure easily calculated and also available on most financial web sites such as Yahoo! Finance. I prefer the operating margin figure, because it is difficult to manipulate under generally accepted accounting principles and gives me a much clearer look at how a company is doing than other figures such as net income (too many nonrecurring items find their way into net income for it to be a reliable yardstick). If a company's operating margin is expanding year over year and quarter over quarter, it indicates that the company is making more money on every dollar of revenue they collect on the goods or services that they sell. Often we find companies that show explosive sales growth but that have poor operating margins. Thus, a company may have lowered prices to stimulate sales, which is great for the top line but isn't a reflection of consistent growth. Other companies, particularly those in the service industries, may show top-line sales, but profits may be eaten up in adding new people and additional marketing costs.

Margins may show a strong but temporary spike for several reasons. First, a company may implement cost controls and reduce expenses so each dollar of sales is bringing a bit more to the bottom line. This is nice, and I am always glad to see the companies I invest in be responsible with the corporate checkbook, but it is not a sustainable source of growth. In retail chains we will often see margins spike when low-sales stores are closed. Again, it's good to see management taking the necessary steps to improve the bottom line, but closing stores is not really the way to grow a company.

The other way in which profit margins expand is where a company sells more of its product but the basic costs of the business do not go up. When Apple's iPod exploded in popularity, the only real cost increase they saw was in the cost to make the new units. Apple's overall SG&A (sales, general, and administrative costs) didn't rise anywhere near as quickly, as its sales and margins exploded to the upside as did the stock.

In Chapter 1, I talked about the eight factors in our model and showed how much each factor has outperformed the market over the past three years. Margin improvement was one of the most successful of all variables over the past few years. Companies that can expand the amount of money on each and every dollar in the door are winning stocks. As productivity has improved over the past 10 years in the United States, with enormous advances in technology and capability, those that are also gaining expansion because of popular products have been rocket ships. As it looks like productivity and technology will continue to grow in the years ahead (I am an optimist and believe that we have a very bright future), the environment for growth stocks in particular should continue.

One of the greatest examples of margin expansion driving stock price growth comes from the world of chickens. Tyson chicken was for many years just a regular chicken processor. They would buy chickens, raise them, dress them out, and sell them to retailers—a decent albeit basic business. However, Tyson began to innovate and find new ways to sell its age-old product and started packaging chicken in different ways. They started selling prepackaged chicken, boneless chicken breasts ready for the grill, frozen chicken dinners, and chicken cut for buffalo wings, among other innovative measures. They found that they could charge more for what was basically the same product. Sales and margins increased. Donald Tyson also noticed that as the economy recovered from the doldrums of the 1970s, Americans began to eat out more frequently. He developed a campaign to sell his product where it was being enjoyed—in restaurants and fast-food joints. One sales call changed the history of chicken. Tyson called on McDonald's Corporation and convinced them to add chicken to the menu—specifically, a new thing called chicken McNuggets. The idea caught on and, because of Tyson's innovative production and marketing techniques, they were the only chicken processor in a position to provide the chicken chunks and were the major supplier for the product that quickly became one of the fastest-selling items on the McDonald's menu. They had a virtual monopoly on the product and were able to charge more without their basic costs rising a bit. Margins expanded and the stock went into a multiyear tear, soaring to new highs and beyond.

I like to give more recent examples of each variable so you can see just how powerful each one is in selecting the right growth stocks. One of the more obvious over the past few years has, of course, been energy and energy-service stocks. The basic cost of running an energy business hasn't really changed, but geopolitical and supply issues have pushed the product price higher. These companies sold the same amount of gas and oil but the margins were much higher. Figure 7.1 shows the price of Suncor in 2005. Margins leaped from 20 percent of sales to over 50 percent and the stock soared 80 percent.

Occidental Petroleum is another great example of the impact of higher-selling prices on profit margins and stock prices. All OXY does is explore for, produce, and market petroleum. From 2003 until 2005, not only did its sales

FIGURE 7.1   Suncor's Performance in 2005

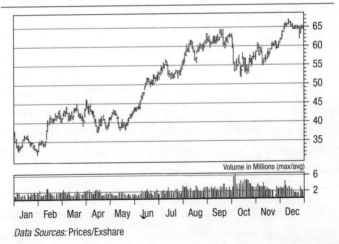

Data Sources: Prices/Exshare

rise quickly, so did its profit margins as the cost of doing business remained fairly stable. Their margins increased each and every year and so did the stock price, growing better than 300 percent in that time frame. The other thing that grew quickly during that time was, of course, the net worth of those who were aware of this expansion.

Another fantastic example comes from the video game world. It's almost impossible to be unaware of the gaming boom. You can play computer games on computers, on special game sets such as Playstation 3, on handheld devices, and even on your cell phone. This boom has meant that manufacturers need graphics-processing chips, the special computer chips that make all the action come alive, from the blood-and-guts games to the high impact of Madden NFL and the popular NBA games. Nvidia was right there and in position to supply the chips that all the gaming manufacturers need. As demand swelled in 2006, their profit margins tripled. So did their stock, up over 100 percent.

We always keep an eye on margins. Rising margins usually mean that a company is dominating its business space or has a new product. Inevitably this will bring competition and margins may begin to erode. We watch for erosion very carefully and keep a close eye on quarter-over-quarter margin growth. There are a lot of reasons profit margins can stop expanding and none of them are good. There may be bloated overhead as management gets too lax as it enjoys its success (a great way to become an ex-manager), or there may be increased regulation in the industry group, as seen in the past, for instance, in the pharmaceuticals and utilities industries. Both of these industries saw margins collapse as government agencies limited what they could charge for their products and forced them to add expensive controls on their factories and plants. Whatever the reason margins stop expanding or even begin collapsing, it is probably a sign that the growth is slowing and it may be time to part company with the stock. Fortunately this will show up in our database model and we will have plenty of warning. On the web site www.getrichwithgrowth.com, you can easily see when the rating for operating margins begins to drop for nearly any stock on Wall Street. You can use this as an early warning indicator and sell before the stock drops.

As long as a company's margins expand, it will be a powerful variable that drives the stock price higher and higher.

Chapter Eight

Let It Flow

~

*A Steady Stream of Cash Leads to a
Steady Stream of Profits.*

THE FIFTH OF OUR EIGHT VARIABLES is **free cash flow**. Recall from Chapter 1 that another one of the most powerful factors in my system is a company's ability to produce free cash flow. From 2004 to 2007, the very best stocks ranked by production of free cash flow outperformed the universe of stocks by 59 percent. Free cash flow is the money that a company has left after paying the cost of doing business and the upkeep and maintenance needed to stay in business. In simple accounting terms, free cash equals operating earnings minus the capital expenditures needed to run the business.

To understand free cash flow, think about your paycheck. You get paid a certain amount, and from that amount expenses such as state and federal income tax, health insurance, Social Security, 401(k) contributions, and such are deducted. What is left are your earnings. If you were a corporation, that is the number you would report to investors as your total earnings. Obviously, if this number rises year after year, you are a more valuable employee, at least on the surface. When you get home and sit down to pay your bills, such as insurance, mortgage or rent, utilities, and food, what is left after these necessary expenses are paid is free cash flow. This is the money you can spend on luxury items, vacations and such, or put into investment accounts. If the number left over is negative, you will have a problem. If you want to do anything else, such as buy clothes, get a haircut, replace the furnace, or even pay for childcare or education, you will need to charge it to your credit cards or take from a home equity loan—just to tread water. Companies face exactly the same scenario. If, after paying their cost of goods sold and basic overhead such as salaries, they have to spend all their earnings to fix and replace old equipment or buildings, for example, they have negative free cash flow and will have to look elsewhere for money to even think about growing the business. If, however, there is plenty of cash left over, it can be spent growing the business.

Free cash flow gives a company a lot of flexibility in its decision making. It can internally finance new ventures or add new product lines and open new markets without going to banks to borrow money or selling additional stock to raise capital. All too often, I have seen companies borrow their way right into failure or sell so many shares that there is no way they can ever earn enough to justify a higher stock price. If a company can't generate free cash flow and become self-financing, it's only a matter of time before the growth is stunted, money can't be borrowed, and the stock price is so low that no one wants to buy another secondary offering. We don't want such poor performers in our portfolio, so we watch free cash flow very carefully.

Free cash flow gives a company the opportunity to do other things as well, all of which are good for investors. It gives companies the ability to pay and raise dividends, for instance. In today's market, this is very important. In days past, growth investors didn't focus on dividends too much as they were more focused on the earnings growth of these stocks. Since Congress enacted dividend tax relief in 2003, dividends are now taxed at just 15 percent on the federal level, which provides investors with more money that can be spent or can be reinvested on a tax-favored basis. Eliminating tax on 85 percent of the dividend automatically made stocks worth more than they were before the act was passed. Amazingly, not only have high-dividend stocks done very well since the act was passed, but the volatility of these stocks has decreased as well. This is Nirvana for a growth investor focusing on fundamentals and risk control, like myself. I view the dividend tax cut as one of the most bullish events in my lifetime and hope that the U.S. Congress has the good sense to renew the credit when it expires in 2010. If they don't, December 2010 could be one of the worst months in stock market history as the market revalues to reflect the increased tax. For now, however, a company's ability to use free cash flow to pay and raise dividends is worth its weight in gold in the stock market.

Companies can also use their free cash flow to buy back stock, another positive development for shareholders. When a company views its own shares as an attractive investment, a couple of really good things happen. First, the number of shares becomes reduced but the earnings and other numbers remain the same. This means the price-to-earnings ratio, PE to growth rate, price to sales, and other key financial ratios will all become lower and attract additional investor interest. We already know that the stock market reacts to supply and demand, and with buybacks companies can both lower the supply and make shares more attractive to investors, thereby raising demand. Stock buybacks are also a powerful psychological factor that demonstrates management's confidence in its abilities and the future. As companies use more and more stock options to compensate executives, the free cash can also be used to buy back stock to offset potential dilution of its shares, also a good move that keeps current shareholders from suffering the ill effects of more shares being issued.

Companies with negative free cash flow, however, have to make some difficult decisions just to keep their operations running. They can borrow money either in a bond offering or from a traditional lending source such as a bank, but both options require incurring an ongoing interest expense that decreases future earnings. To offset increased costs (interest payments), a company will have to earn a high rate of return on the borrowed capital to offset these new expenses. A company can also issue new stock to finance operations, making existing shareholder stakes worth less than before. Thus, unless the company earns more to offset the dilutive effects, investors will eventually sell their shares en masse, which will drive down the price, which will lead to more selling. We saw a lot of this during the dot-com boom, when companies reported eye-popping earnings growth but consumed cash faster than they had any hope of outgrowing. These companies continued to sell stock to finance their seemingly wonderful growth. Once enthusiasm waned (because they weren't making money!) and they couldn't sell shares to further finance their operations, many of them went out of business in the blink of an eye. This is not a scenario we want to see in our growth stock portfolio.

Companies can also raise funds by cutting expenses, and one cost-cutting measure often employed is to reduce or eliminate their dividend payments. Just as a dividend increase is good for investors, a dividend cut is usually not a happy event for stockholders.

I do not have to look any further than my stock-rating database to see some examples of just how powerful the ability to generate free cash flow can be. One of the unique features of my database tool is that it gives me the ability to rank stocks by any of our fundamental eight variables—including free cash flow. In January 2007, I searched for some of the top free cash flow stocks on Wall Street. Take, for example, PW Eagle, a stock I liked a lot in early 2007. PW Eagle, Inc. engages in the manufacture and distribution of polyvinyl chloride (PVC) pipe and fittings in the United States. Starting in 2005, Eagle's business started expanding with the boom in the real estate market and they began to produce huge piles of free cash flow, a lot of which has gone to buy back stocks. The stock exploded in 2006, moving from around $8 a share to well over $30. Since they work with municipal water plants as well as the residential building industry, and we are at the start of a large rebuilding and retooling of water plants initiative across the country, Eagle should be able to keep growing that pile of cash for the benefit of shareholders.

Another great example of free cash flow at work is Holly Corporation, which I began buying in October 2004. I still own shares of Holly in my newsletter portfolios. So far, we're up 430 percent. Holly Corporation is in the business of refining, transporting, terminaling, and marketing petroleum products and they also manufacture and market asphalt products from various terminals in Arizona and New Mexico. They regularly produce far more money than it costs to run and maintain the business and have used the cash to better than double the dividend since 2003 and buy back over 6 million shares. The net result of using free cash flow to pay dividends and buy back stock is that the stock went from around $7 a share to over $35 in January 2006!

Analyzing the free cash flow situation of a company is no different from examining your personal finances. If you have extra money after you pay your expenses, you can invest it to build your wealth, buy your wife a necklace, go out to dinner, and enjoy the good things in life. If you have limited or no free cash flow, you have a problem and will have to make tough choices: Cut expenses or borrow, sometimes to the point of bankruptcy if you aren't able to earn more or spend less. Companies with free cash flow have the ability to grow the business, open new stores, develop exciting new products to increase profits, and reward shareholders with dividends, stock buybacks, and higher stock prices. The rich get richer. By paying attention to free cash flow, we can as well.

Chapter Nine

It's All Variable

~

*It Takes Precision Tuning to
Target Today's Best Stocks.*

So far, we have examined five key variables critical to helping you uncover today's best growth stocks:

1. Earnings revisions
2. Earnings surprises
3. Sales growth
4. Profit margin expansion
5. Free cash flow

As you know, I use an eight-factor fundamental formula to target the crème de la crème of Wall Street stocks. I am pretty sure that by now you are starting to get a good idea of how these eight factors exert a tremendous influence on a company's financial condition and ultimately its stock price. So, pay close attention—I'll soon show you how to apply the complete formula to your own investments. Plus, I'll give you a turn at the helm of my actual stock-rating database. But first, let's review each of the remaining three variables in our formula. Now that you understand the first five, these remaining variables are pretty straightforward and easy to explain, so I'll cover all three in this one chapter. I will describe each of them and why they are important and give an example of each in action so you can see for yourself how powerfully these variables can impact the price of a stock.

As I have explained, any single fundamental variable might work for a period of time and then all of a sudden stop doing well. In the 1970s, book value was a key determination of future strong returns. In the takeover-crazy 1980s, interest coverage and earnings before interest, taxes, depreciation, and amortization (EBITDA) was one of the key variables. These things change over time and can change very quickly. There will be times when stocks with earnings surprises are all the rage, and others when sales growth (such as the late 1990s) is the hot button that sends stocks higher. By paying attention to all eight of the variables that are linked to stock price performance, we can assure ourselves that no matter what today's hot button is, we will identify the stocks that will be influenced by the trend. As a bonus, since we still include the other variables in addition to whatever the flavor of the month is, we will own only the highest-quality stocks in the group.

The first of the three remaining variables, and the most common fundamental variable, is **earnings growth**. All we are looking for here is growth in reported earnings quarter after quarter and year after year. Every quarter, companies release a report of how well they have done for the prior three months, how much stuff they bought, how much they spent, and how much money they made. The net result is reported in the company's earnings per share (EPS). It is a simple matter to derive this number: It's just the total profit for the quarter minus any preferred stock dividends divided by the total number of shares outstanding. The number will tell us whether earnings are growing at a strong clip year over year. Stocks are ultimately priced on earnings, because the markets place a huge emphasis on the EPS numbers every quarter. A company with higher year-over-year earnings is automatically worth a little bit more each time it reports, and generally the stock price will move higher to reflect this fact. America Movil, the Mexican telecommunications and wireless company, has been a great example of the type of steady growth in earnings that we look for when picking growth stocks for the long haul. As America Movil reports earnings that are higher year after year, the stock is worth more year after year. Since 2004, the stock has shot up 300 percent.

Another great example of steady earnings growth attracting attention and driving stock prices higher is Google. Starting in mid-2005, Google began reporting a string of ever-higher earnings, quarter after quarter after quarter. As a result, the stock came under heavy buying pressure and has moved up 70 percent in a nice orderly fashion ever since. (See Figure 9.1.)

Not only do we want to see earnings be higher year over year; we like to see them up even more this quarter

FIGURE 9.1   Google's Mid-2005 to May 2007 Performance

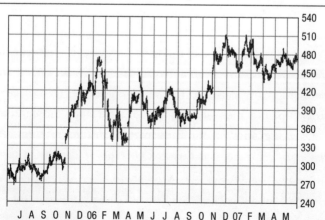

compared with the same period the prior year. If earnings year over year were up 10 percent during the last quarter, we want to see them up more than that this quarter. This is where our next variable, **earnings momentum**, plays into our formula. For a stock to rank high on the variable, it needs to show a steady string of accelerating earnings each and every quarter. There are times when this is easily one of the most important variables in the model. When the market is in a strong bull run, earnings momentum is one of the biggest driving forces behind stock prices. There is a whole school of investing and even a large daily financial newspaper, namely *Investor's Business Daily*®, devoted to investing based on earnings momentum and other important fundamental variables. In addition, dozens of mutual funds and hedge funds utilize earnings momentum as their primary basis for trading and investing.

Earlier I explained that folks with large piles of lovely cash can pile into a stock and create positive returns as the stock attracts persistent buying pressure. Since we know they love earnings momentum and they can drive a stock up in a nice orderly fashion, earnings momentum plays a big part in our fundamental grading system. A really nice example of this is Centerpoint Energy, a top-rated stock in mid-2007. Centerpoint makes an especially strong example, because although most people tend to think of sexy, hot companies that are discussed on the financial news shows and featured in magazine and newspaper and web site headlines, Centerpoint Energy is anything but hot and rarely gets mentioned anywhere. The odds of hearing about the company at a cocktail party or on the golf course are pretty slim. Centerpoint sells electricity and natural gas. They pay a nice dividend. But looking under the hood of the earnings report is a little like realizing that a nondescript car is really a high horsepower racing car. As you can see in Figure 9.2, Centerpoint has continually accelerated its earnings in 2006 and the stock has handsomely rewarded investors who noticed.

FIGURE 9.2   Centerpoint Energy EPS

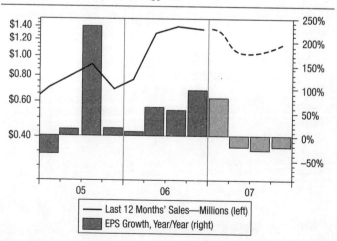

— Last 12 Months' Sales—Millions (left)
  EPS Growth, Year/Year (right)

To see the impact of large pools of money held by hedge funds and mutual fund folks, look at Figure 9.3, which shows monthly prices of Maidenform Company. Maidenform may have sexier products than energy, but it is basically a fairly simple company without a lot of buzz and excitement around the stock. As their earnings growth accelerated in late 2005 and early 2006, the volume surged and sent the stock up well over 100 percent in a very short period of time.

The final variable in our eight-part formula is **return on equity**. This is a critically important number and one of the most watched, not just by me but by most investors. Return on equity (ROE) measures the rate of return

FIGURE 9.3   Maidenform EPS

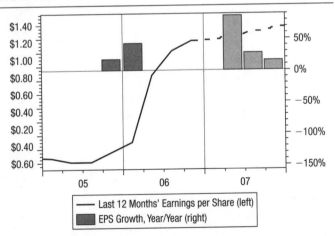

Last 12 Months' Earnings per Share (left)
EPS Growth, Year/Year (right)

management is earning on the shareholders' invested cash. ROE is determined by dividing net income by shareholders' equity. The information revealed is powerful stuff. ROE can tell us just how effectively the company is using the cash it generates from the business. I like to see ROE start out high and get higher. If the ROE rate is growing, then I know management is making effective upgrades and investments that will increase the return on the money I have invested with the company. If it turns lower, then perhaps it is not using the money as wisely as I would like.

A company that earns high returns on shareholder money is far less likely to do things that will erode value, like announce a new stock offering or borrow money to keep the business going, both of which are typically negative events for current shareholders. I want to know that the company is capable of generating the funds it needs from its day-to-day operations and has some cash left over to grow the business. A company that has a very high return on the dollars that have been invested is more likely to produce strong free cash flow.

A company's ROE should be compared across industry groups and not the entire universe of stocks. A consulting firm may well have a very high return on equity simply because it has no real asset base. All of the money is spent on advertising and marketing, as well as opening new offices. These things do not show up in the equity column. Comparing the ROE of a consulting firm to, say, a steel manufacturer that has enormous equity investments in factories, land, and raw material is not really a fair comparison. So keep an eye on how a company's ROE measures up against the same type of company and don't compare apples to aardvarks.

I cannot emphasize enough that you need to use all of the variables we've examined when seeking market-beating growth stocks to add to your portfolio. Fads in the market can change quicker than a summer storm can blow in off the Atlantic in South Florida. By using all of these important variables, you can be assured that by the time the storm hits you will have found shelter (by selling those dead-weight stocks in your portfolio) and be ready to take advantage of the sunshine that is sure to follow.

Chapter Ten

Know Your Alpha Beta

There Is a Secret Sauce. How to Measure the Ingredients.

IF THE WORLD WERE A PERFECT place, once we had a basket of stocks that had strong fundamentals, we would be able to sit back, relax, and watch our profits pile up. But the real world is not a perfect place and Wall Street is even less so. The markets have two attributes that can have a substantial impact on our investment portfolio. First, the stock markets have all the psychological symptoms of your average severe schizophrenic. Second, the stock market is the ultimate supply-and-demand marketplace, and opinions on the attractiveness or unattractiveness of a particular company can have overwhelming impact on our performance. The reality is that good companies with sound business models and profits can be unduly and harshly punished in the short run even if they are long-term winners. For this reason, I think it makes sense to continually measure our stocks in terms of their *risk and reward* characteristics as well as their fundamental strengths.

The first risk/reward measure that I examine is known in mathematical terms as *beta*. Beta simply measures how a stock moves in tandem with the market. This is often referred to as *systematic risk*, which is the sensitivity of a stock to the movements of an entire stock market benchmark. Beta attempts to measure the movement of a specific asset relative to the broad market. A beta of 1 implies that you can expect the movement of a stock to match that of the benchmark and essentially move in tandem with the benchmark. In other words, if a stock or portfolio had a beta of 1.10, it can be said that the asset has historically moved higher and lower than the market by 10 percent. Similarly, if an asset has a beta of 0.80, then it has historically moved 20 percent less than the market, both up and down. Beta is determined using *regression analysis*—a statistical methodology that attempts to determine the strength of a relationship between one dependent variable (the individual stock) and a series of other changing variables (the stock market).

For example, if the stock market goes up 10 percent and shares of BlueChip Incorporated also go up 10 percent, the BlueChip shares are said to have a beta of 1, a perfect match to the market. It the market goes up by 10 percent and shares of Exciting New Stuff Co. rise by 30 percent, the Exciting New Stuff shares would have a beta of 3. It doesn't matter if the movement is up or down in the overall market; we are just measuring the relationship between the individual stock and the stock market benchmark as a whole.

When we look at the type of stocks to own, low-beta stocks tend to be the very-low-risk, less-volatile stocks such as electric utilities, some banks, and large blue-chip stocks. As we venture into more aggressive, less sure companies, betas will tend to rise. I try to minimize beta across my portfolio by mixing and matching high- and low-beta stocks to minimize the effect of the overall market movement on my portfolios. This hopefully allows us to be in control of our own destiny, by picking a balanced portfolio of stocks that have sound fundamental characteristics that are not overly impacted by day-to-day market fluctuations. As a numbers person, I like exerting more control (or at least less chaos) than what is offered by leaving my financial fate to the fickle moods swings of Wall Street.

The other type of risk we have to face is called *unsystematic risk*. In finance, this is defined as risk that is random and uncorrelated to the overall stock market. It might be news that affects only one company, such as lowered earnings estimates, or conditions that impact just a single group of companies in the same business, such as new regulations or market constraints. It is very difficult to protect against unsystematic risk, so the higher a stock's unsystematic risk, the more you need to diversify. For example, I look at less diversification with more liquid, large-capitalization stocks with low unsystematic risk than I would with less liquid, micro- and small-capitalization stocks with higher unsystematic risk. To reduce an overall portfolio's unsystematic risk, we must spread our investment capital over stocks in different industries, in stocks that are affected differently by economic factors, as well as stocks with different beta characteristics.

My portfolios are constructed by the use of careful measurements that mix and match different betas to diversify away as much unsystematic risk as possible. Such an approach is vital if we are to achieve "get rich" results. With a selection of fundamentally powerful companies in our portfolio, the one thing we do not want is for market movements or industry or individual company events to take away from the incredible potential our models give us. I cannot emphasize enough how important risk control is to achieving smooth, steady returns.

Beta protects us on the downside. But my most important performance measurement, which is really the secret sauce, is *alpha*. There is no doubt that alpha has been crucial to my success in the stock market. Alpha is the measurement of how much of a stock's price performance is due to nonmarket influences. Usually, alphas are attributable to strong fundamentals and the financial performance of a company. Alpha, in its simplest term, is the measurement of excess return above the stock's most appropriate stock market benchmark. So, every stock has an alpha and a beta. Beta is that portion of the stock price due to the overall market, and alpha is anything in excess of that return. One might say that all stocks are like dogs but only alpha gets the dog to the winner's circle at Westminster Kennel Club.

I first became aware of this very powerful predictive measure more than 27 years ago. I was in college studying finance and the markets. In those days (and it hasn't changed that much today), we were taught that it was impossible to beat the return of the overall stock market without incurring additional risk. Most of the investment theory at the time suggested that you were much better off putting your money in funds that mirrored the Standard & Poor's 500 (S&P 500) or another relevant index. Wells Fargo was one of the leading advocates of this approach, and I was fortunate to have a professor from Wells Fargo who worked with students to research the efficient markets approach. Wells Fargo got very cheap (i.e., free) mathematical labor from myself and others who experimented with Wells Fargo's mainframe computer. In return, I received access to a wealth of stock price and financial data, which was a big deal back in the 1970s before the Internet and laptops made such data widely available.

One of my biggest projects as a fledgling quantitative analyst was to build a model for my Wells Fargo professor that mirrored the S&P 500 using less than 500 stocks. I attempted to generate the precise conditions that would mirror the index with the same level of risk and same industry weightings but with a group of stocks that would precisely *track* the S&P 500. That was the goal, anyway. When I built my first portfolio of 332 stocks that was designed to mirror the S&P 500, I found to my surprise that this portfolio accidentally beat the market! This was quite a shock to one who had been taught that this was impossible, so I got to work dissecting what had created this stock market anomaly.

The rest of my career ensued because of what I discovered. Within this initial portfolio of 332 stocks, there were a select group of stocks that continually and substantially outperformed the market as a whole with the same and in some cases less risk. My career and investment life changed on the spot. I had uncovered the stocks with high alphas! These high-alpha stocks tended to move independently of the overall stock market index and were much more likely to offer better returns going forward than other stocks.

Once I understood that stocks with high alphas out-perform the market and would give me the opportunity to earn returns far in excess of what passive index fund investing offered, I began to study what caused stocks to have high alphas. I found two reasons for the outsized per-formance. First, some stocks were fundamentally unsound and were sold short by professionals betting the stock would go down. When the short sellers began to buy back stock to lock in their profits, these not-so-wonderful com-panies would experience an explosive rally. This often happens near short-term stock market bottoms, as we saw in April 2001 and October 2001 when some technology stocks skyrocketed due to short-covering rallies.

The second reason for high alpha is due to buying pressure. Institutions and individuals recognize the power-ful fundamental performance of a group of stocks and they buy them heavily. As we know, the stock market, like any other market, responds to supply and demand. Increased demand pushes stocks higher and higher relative to their respective indexes.

Today, we hear much about *high-alpha stocks* from market pundits and gurus. Amazingly, many of them use the term completely incorrectly. First, they calculate the alpha as well as the beta against just the S&P 500—for every stock. However, if the stock isn't in the S&P 500, but is instead in the NASDAQ Composite, the more accurate calculation would use the NASDAQ benchmark or other index that the stock is more correlated to and tracks more precisely. The reason that correlation is so important is that the higher the correlation, the more statistically significant the alpha and beta. But if you compare a stock to a low-correlating stock market benchmark, you are essentially getting a statistically poor alpha and beta, or what I like to call "garbage in, garbage out." Let me explain it another way. Let's say you compare a small-capitalization stock to the S&P 500. You are essentially comparing a Chihuahua to an elephant. They may both have four legs and a tail, but they behave very differently! A stock that appears to have high alpha relative to a blue-chip index might not when calculated against the higher-powered NASDAQ index.

The second major error I often see takes place when the analyst uses relative strength and calls it alpha. *Relative strength* measures how a stock is doing relative to the index at any moment. For example, if a stock tracks a market benchmark precisely with 100 percent correlation, and that benchmark rises 50 percent in a year while the stock rises 100 percent, that stock will end up having a beta of 2 and an alpha of 0. Now, I know what you are thinking: How can a stock that does double the overall stock market have an alpha of 0? It's simple: The entire stock return was completely explained by its high beta and none was explained by its alpha. Essentially, high-alpha stocks often zig when the overall stock market zags. Also, I like to keep my betas as low as possible so I can reduce my dependence on the overall stock market and control my own destiny by focusing on each particular stock's performance.

In other words, high-relative-strength and high-beta stocks will all too often flame out and crash and burn when the overall stock market turns sour. Alpha is measured over a longer period of time (trailing 52 weeks) and is created by genuine buying pressure. It is not impacted by short-term price movements. Indeed, many of my higher-alpha stocks tend to zig when the market zags and perform exactly the opposite.

So there is my alpha-and-beta story about growth stock investing. Just as we memorized our ABCs as a building block to learning to read and write, learning our alphas and betas puts us on the path to reading stock performance more clearly and, hopefully, investment success. If we stick to companies with sound fundamentals that have genuine persistent buying pressure, manage our betas so market fluctuations don't have an overly large impact, and diversify away risk, we are well on the way to the wealth-building results we hope to achieve.

Of course, I don't expect you to have to figure this all out on your own. In Chapter 13, I'll give you complete instructions, as well as hands-on access to my stock-rating database, which can do it all for you.

Chapter Eleven

Don't Be a Deviant

——— ❧ ———

*Deviance Is No More Appreciated
in the Stock Market Than Anywhere
Else in Life.*

WHILE WE'VE COVERED the important topic of alpha and touched on risk versus reward, we need to delve into the concepts a bit deeper. I frequently hear a lot of talk by professional and individual investors about risk versus reward, but few of them offer a meaningful way to measure either. Some folks will point to various prices where they think that the risk for lower prices is higher or identify a price at which they think prices could rise, but this is poor guidance. As a numbers person, I knew that there had to be a better way to quantify and measure risk and reward, so I went looking for the answer and believe I have found it.

I do not want to sound like too much of a math geek, but a little explanation is necessary. *Quantitative analysis* is nothing more than applying mathematical theory to the movement of stock prices. We can chart stock movements and apply a series of statistical measurements to see how prices move in relationship to underlying market forces. Previously, I introduced you to the concepts of alpha and beta and how these measure each stock's movement relative to the appropriate stock market benchmark.

Now I'll introduce another character, a shady fellow who represents the *excessive risk* that needs to be avoided when owning growth stocks as measured by standard deviation or statistical variance. *Standard deviation* measures just how much a stock wiggles based on its trading range. When a stock's price movement is too jerky and erratic—or volatile—it's clearly a sign of bad things to come and needs to be avoided. That's what standard deviation and my reward-to-risk measures help spot. In basic form, we divide a stock's alpha (the return independent of the stock market that typically comes from buying pressure) by its standard deviation. We measure this over a 52-week period as we do with all our statistical measures. Any longer time frame than that is essentially too far back in the past and becomes less meaningful. For example, many quantitative analysts on Wall Street utilize five-year risk-and-reward measurements, but I think that's just too long. What does price movement from five years ago have to do with today? That's too far back in the past and would lead to measuring movement in different economic and market environments with little impact on today's stock prices. My calculation gives us a number that I call the *reward/risk ratio* that determines my *quantitative grade*. Stocks with good reward/risk ratios tend to be lower-risk stocks that are just plugging away, earning excess returns in a smooth consistent manner. These are the ones with the high quantitative grades that we want to own.

We recalculate these reward/risk measurements (e.g., alpha, beta, standard deviation, etc.) every weekend for every stock in my database. That's almost 5,000 stocks. Any stock that trades 5,000 shares per day and has been trading for the past 52 weeks qualifies to be in my database, so illiquid stocks and initial public offerings will be excluded.

In order to always keep the best stocks in our portfolio we have to be fairly diligent in determining when reward and risk ratings change. Sometimes you will see a stock rise dramatically in a very short period of time and the risk scores will get progressively worse and we need to sell the stock. This was the case with the energy stocks we had previously identified as good growth performers. We began to sell them even though they continued to rise in price because they had become just too volatile to continue to hold. On the flipside, there will be times that a stock gets slammed because of missed earnings or other one-off events and then settles down and becomes far less risky than it was before it fell in price.

My approach to measuring reward and risk is unique. Conventional wisdom holds that the market is efficient and extra reward will be gained only by taking on extra risk. But by focusing on stocks with high alphas and low standard deviation, we can actually have our cake and eat it, too, by getting extra reward with less risk. Our approach is unique because of the time frame we use to measure the variance. We have found that 52 weeks is the best time frame in which to do these weekly studies, due largely to the fact that the stock market has many seasonal characteristics, such as the January Effect, the Sell-in-May-and-Go-Away crowd, holiday sales, and so on. I should add that we continually test longer and shorter periods and always will, but 52 weeks has unquestionably stood the test of time.

Okay, I know what you are thinking. "That's great for you. You have an advanced math degree, a staff of 50, and a lot of high-end computing power." Maybe you have an English degree and a laptop that is dominated by a teenage daughter who spends every waking minute on Myspace or a 12-year old son who is now on the 903rd level of his Soldiers of Fortune video game. How could you do all these calculations and determine the reward/risk characteristics for the stocks in your portfolio? The short answer is that you probably can't, which is why we've created the companion web site to this book so that you can enjoy using the same database I use with the statistical measurements done for you—provided in clearly stated letter-grade ratings. Here (www.getrichwithgrowth.com) you can enter a stock symbol and, in addition to my *eight fundamental variable rankings,* you will find my *quantitative grade* for each stock: *A* is a Strong Buy, *B* is a Buy, *C* is a Hold, *D* is a Sell, and *F* is a Strong Sell. But I'm getting ahead of myself. Right now, I want to show you the power of my *reward/risk ratio,* and how it can lead you to greater, safer profits.

It's important to note that when we measure the reward, or *alpha,* we look for stocks that have true alpha and are moving independent of the overall stock market so we will be less dependent on the overall stock market for our success. Sometimes stocks will rise due to short covering or being hyped and touted by Wall Street. These are *not* the stocks we want to own. We want to own stocks with sound fundamentals that attract persistent institutional buying pressure. Think about this for a second.

According to the Investment Company Institute's web site, U.S. hedge funds alone have over $10 trillion at their disposal. Exchange-traded funds have another trillion or so. Hedge funds have many hundreds of billions of dollars and they use leverage to increase their buying power. We have already talked about how Wall Street has a herd instinct. When a stock that has great fundamentals begins to get noticed by the big funds and they turn that incredible stack of cash in the stock's direction, it begins to move up in a fairly steady progression week after week. As a stock attracts more and more attention, more and more of Wall Street's treasure chest is diverted into its shares and the move up is smooth. A great sign of a high-alpha stock is one that has created so much buying pressure that market movement is almost irrelevant. The big boys want the stock and they are going to buy regardless of the day-to-day gyrations of the stock market. Even when the market is down, our high-alpha stocks are often up.

When the move first starts, it is a very smooth price progression. We consider this type of stock to be very conservative in nature. When stocks like eBay and Google were starting their tremendous price runs, many investment professionals considered them to be high risk. Frankly, in the early stages of their run, such as eBay in 2003 or Google in 2005 before it was added to the S&P 500, my system indicated that these stocks were safe due to the tremendous institutional buying pressure under these stocks, which created a high alpha combined with low volatility. These stocks had great reward/risk characteristics and received a quantitative *A* grade from us as a result.

Our work indicated also that both eBay and Google, when they were surging in 2003 and 2004, respectively, had high fundamental grades in addition to their good reward/risk characteristics. Therefore, we classified both eBay and Google as *conservative* stocks in the early stages of their respective rallies. As their rallies progressed, their reward/risk ratios weakened a bit as the stocks became riskier. This scenario typically happens when the institutional buying pressure under a popular stock becomes erratic, which is exactly what happened to eBay and Google in 2004 and 2005, respectively, when we downgraded the stocks to a quantitative *B* grade. When this happens, we consider the stock to be *moderately aggressive*. Eventually, as eBay decayed in early 2005, it was quickly reclassified as *aggressive* by my system and subsequently downgraded to a quantitative *C* and then *D*, and eventually received an *F* grade.

Here is an interesting point: The primary reason that eBay flamed out in early 2005 was that the folks at McGraw-Hill who are tasked with identifying which stocks will make up the S&P 500 decided to trim eBay's weight (and 99 other of the largest stocks in the S&P 500) by throwing out all their insider shares in what was called the *free-float adjustment*. Specifically, from mid-March to mid-September 2005, the 100 largest companies in the S&P 500 performed poorly due to persistent institutional selling pressure that occurred in the six-month period because index funds had to adjust their holdings accordingly. My quantitative grade warned us of the institutional selling pressure that was caused by the S&P 500's free-float adjustment. Ironically, the reason Google was not hurt by the S&P 500's free-float adjustment, unlike eBay, Qualcomm, and other stocks, is that it was not part of the S&P 500 when the adjustment started in mid-March 2005.

I hope that you now have a better appreciation of the *lifecycle* of a stock and how my quantitative grade for a stock changes during its lifetime. What might be considered a conservative stock with a quantitative *A* grade today will typically become more volatile over time as the institutional buying pressure becomes more erratic and then will often be reclassified as a moderately aggressive stock with a quantitative *B* grade. Eventually, as the institutional buying pressure dissipates, a quantitative *C* grade will follow. Those stocks with persistent institutional selling pressure typically receive a quantitative *D* or *F* grade and are often classified as aggressive stocks.

Another way to explain how stocks can receive an *A* grade and then slip to a *B*, *C*, *D*, or *F* grade is like having a friend over for cocktail hour. If your friend has one beer, odds are that he is fine and there is little risk in his walking or driving home. However, if he drinks two or three beers, he may start acting more erratically and you may have to escort him home or take his car keys. If he drinks all the beer in your refrigerator and sneaks a few shots of scotch while you are not looking, his behavior will likely become increasingly erratic and his ability to walk straight (e.g., standard deviation) will likely be severely compromised.

For a good real-life example, let's look more closely at eBay from 2003 to 2005. In March 2003, eBay became a buy in our portfolios. It had high scores on all the fundamental variables and the reward/risk ratio showed it to be a tremendous opportunity. The stock stayed an *A* in my stock-grading system. As we entered December, the selling pressure abated and the big money started coming back to eBay, giving it an *A* score again early in the month. As the big funds put more money down for eBay the stock went on a tear, rising almost 40 percent very quickly until scores slipped again in March, and it remained a *B* until May. Then, the money poured back in as fundamentals continued to surprise on the upside and the stock shot ahead 25 percent in two months. Those who owned only

A-graded stocks (and had no tax considerations where capital gains are concerned) in their portfolio were invested in eBay with relatively smooth returns. Conservative investors who held *A*- and *B*-ranked stocks had only a two-year investment in the shares, better than doubling their money along the way. As the rating continued to slip, we stopped suggesting the stock in our portfolios and sold our shares. As Figure 11.1 shows, once the stock turned to a *C* grade and eventually a *D*, selling pressure replaced buying pressure and the shares went south pretty quickly.

FIGURE 11.1   eBay's Lifecycle, 2003–2005

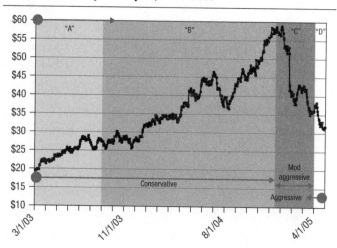

Utilizing these important quantitative tools will set you apart from other growth investors. It's not enough to invest your hard-earned money based solely on the fundamentals, since if no one is buying the stock it may just sit there and look stupid. Or even worse, the folks that make up the major stock indexes, like the S&P 500, can jerk stocks around by messing with their indexes (and they do this more frequently than you may realize). A high quantitative grade is typically indicative of institutional buying pressure and critical for success. Obviously, you have to know where you are on the reward/risk cycle at all times— eBay is great example of this. The company revolutionized the way people buy things and helped millions of people clean out their garage and attic at a profit. There are people who quit their jobs just to sell stuff on eBay. In fact, the shelves in the business section of the bookstore are crowded with how-to-sell-on-eBay books. There is no doubt that eBay is a revolutionary company, but if the folks at McGraw-Hill that maintain the S&P 500 want to trim eBay or add Google, they can jerk these stocks around.

No matter how strongly you feel about a company, there will likely be times when it becomes too risky to own. Institutional investors around the world have a herd mentality, and if the big institutional investors are tripping over themselves to sell a stock, you could get steamrolled if a stock has poor reward/risk characteristics with a quantitative D or F grade. Buying such stocks is like running to meet the bulls in Pamplona, Spain. You will undoubtedly get stepped on! Being of Basque descent, I like to go with the flow rather than swim against the tide (or run head first into charging bulls).

When big institutions dump stocks to lock in profits or dress their portfolios for quarterly reports, you should stay out of their way. When powerful buying pressure slips and a stock starts experiencing heavy selling, my quantitative grades will decline. This is because the volatility (i.e., standard deviation) tends to rise and the reward/risk characteristics tend to decay.

Under no circumstances do you want to wait to sell a stock. One of the worst feelings in the world is to own a great stock like eBay or Qualcomm and to have it double, only to give back all your gains. If you pay attention to the institutional buying pressure underneath a stock and its related risk level, you will always know when to get out of a stock. This way you will very seldom, if ever, sell a stock at the wrong time. Although I do not have the time or space to teach you the calculations needed to calculate my proprietary quantitative grades, I am more than happy to share them with you. At our companion web site, all you have to do is enter the ticker symbol and you'll receive the current quantitative grade for nearly any stock on Wall Street. Thanks to my database, you now have the same tools that I have developed over the past 27 years! As a result, you do not need to get stressed about each individual stock, since the web site tells you the reward/ risk characteristics for all the stocks in your portfolio.

Chapter Twelve

The Zigzag Approach

*Go in Different Directions to Stay
on the Profit Track.*

ONE OF THE MORE IMPORTANT things I try to do when putting together a portfolio of growth stocks is to neutralize the market risk, or *beta*, of my portfolio. The biggest tool I have to achieve this is something a math geek like myself calls *co-variance*. In layperson's terms, this means that I try to find stocks that *zig* when others *zag*. In statistics, co-variance is used to measure how two separate variables relate to each other over time. In the stock market, co-variance is used to describe how two stocks move in relation to each other across different time frames and in different types of market environments. I call this the *zigzag approach to investing*. Specifically, I want to have some stocks in my portfolio that zig in response to market and economic events, while others zag on the same news.

Because I am a numbers person and computer geek, I use *optimization models* that help me find stocks that zig when the market zags. Specifically, an optimization model takes a bunch of stocks (i.e., squiggly lines on the computer screen) and tries to figure out how to optimally combine these stocks to achieve the lowest possible risk (i.e., make a smooth line). The computing power is helpful, but in reality a lot of the analysis comes down to common sense that says that a portfolio should be diversified across different industries and risk categories. When you do your screening and develop a list of stocks that have great fundamentals and high reward/risk characteristics, then it is time to do a little mixing and matching to select the best stocks to buy. If you see that a lot of the stocks you screened for are in one industry group, then pick a few of the very best and offset them with a group of stocks from a different industry that will respond differently to market and economic conditions.

Let's look at an example of how you might do this. One of the stocks my database has identified as a good pick has been America Movil, the Mexican telecommunications company. America Movil has been a great stock for us and I think it will continue to be strong for some time. The stock responds primarily to events related to Latin America and the specifics of the cellular industry. As you can see in Figure 12.1, the stock jumps around a lot as it continues to climb higher as events unfold.

Another stock my database identified was Schlumberger, an oil-services company. Its price will respond to events and news related to the specifics of oil exploration and drilling, as well as geopolitical events related to oil prices. Figure 12.2 shows how the stock price moves around over time, responding to industry- and company-specific events.

FIGURE 12.1   America Movil 2006 Performance

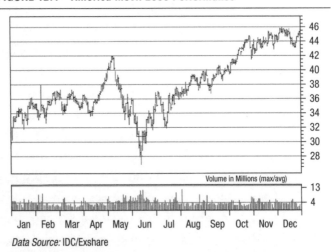

Data Source: IDC/Exshare

FIGURE 12.2   Schlumberger 2006 Performance

Data Source: IDC/Exshare

Finally, let's look at Google (Figure 12.3), the premier technology stock of the past few years. Its stock price responds to events in the search industry and the flow of Internet advertising dollars. It jumps around in price just as the other two stocks do, based on events that tend to impact a tech stock.

If you focus on the individual day-to-day movement of stock prices, it can have you jumping around the room and banging gongs and pushing buzzers like a certain financial television talk show host—all good fun but it won't necessarily make you rich. But let's take these three high-return, volatile growth stocks and look at them as a portfolio. As

FIGURE 12.3   Google 2006 Performance

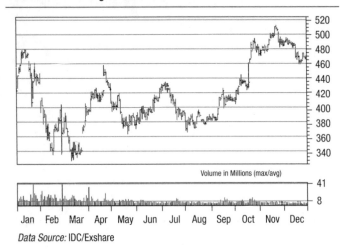

Data Source: IDC/Exshare

you can see in Figure 12.4, by combining these three stocks into a portfolio, they zig and zag in different directions at different times, and the overall performance line is much smoother when the three stocks are combined than when any of them stand alone. The combination of these kinds of stocks and the resulting smoother, less volatile line is what we seek to create, and that will make us rich.

When you put together a growth stock portfolio that can take you down the road to becoming rich, keep the zigzag approach in mind. Look for ways to mix and match stocks that insulate your total portfolio from as much market-specific risk as possible. For example, if you have a bunch of retail stocks in your portfolio that have a

FIGURE 12.4   AMX, SLB, and GOOG Combined Performance

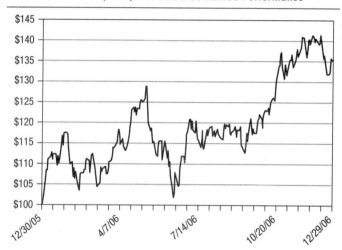

tendency to do very well when the economy is strong, try to have a few that tend to do well when economic conditions slow. Drugs, utilities, and food stocks would probably fill the bill nicely in this situation.

It's important that you stick to the fundamentals of growth stock investing. Find companies in different industry groups so you can create a zigzag portfolio, but make sure the stocks you select have strong fundamentals and great quantitative grades. For example, technology stocks are affected by an entirely different set of circumstances than those that impact financial companies, so if you have Google, you might want to add some shares of Goldman Sachs to better achieve the zigzag effect. Both are great companies and both had the superior fundamental and quantitative characteristics of winning stocks as of mid-2007 according to my database, but they respond differently to market and economic conditions. As a result, they zig and zag relative to each other and help to effectively smooth overall portfolio volatility.

If you are comfortable with spreadsheet programs such as Microsoft Excel, you can determine how different stocks correlate to each other. The price data from sites like Yahoo! Finance is easy to download into a spreadsheet, and, best of all, it's free! However, I have a much better solution. Let me give you a short-cut to utilizing expensive optimization models. When I ask my optimization model to achieve a high return with the lowest possible volatility (e.g., standard deviation), it typically comes back with a recommendation of 60 percent in conservative stocks, 30 percent in moderately aggressive stocks, and 10 percent in aggressive stocks (and I sort my buy lists in my monthly newsletters in this manner). My 60/30/10 mix provides for smoother, steadier returns. On our companion web site, just click on each stock and you will get an in-depth profile on the stock, plus it will tell you whether a stock is conservative, moderately aggressive, or aggressive based on its volatility (i.e., standard deviation).

Another aspect to my zigzag approach is to find and own a few of what I like to call *oasis stocks* in my portfolio.

These are stocks that will do well when there is an overall calamity in the market and in the world. I usually tend to have some defense stocks with great fundamental and quantitative grades, because they tend to do very well in times of political crisis and international tension, such as Iran's nuclear defiance. Food and tobacco stocks tend to hold up very well when the economy goes into a prolonged slowdown. Stocks that pay high dividends and meet all the other criteria also tend to do well in falling markets, especially since the passage of dividend tax relief, because most dividends are taxed at only 15 percent on the federal level. I call these *oasis* stocks, because I can almost always count on them when something bad happens or something hits the fan. I will have a few of these resilient oasis stocks in the mix to make sure that my portfolio is zigging when the rest of the world is zagging.

The 60/30/10 mix in conservative, moderately aggressive, and aggressive stocks, respectively, is a very important part of keeping performance on the smooth track to riches and not getting derailed by taking excessive risk. When the stock market is soft, the resilient nature of the 60 percent in conservative stocks will more than offset the weakness of the more aggressive stocks in your portfolio. When the stock market is running smoothly, we should get smooth, steady growth from all the respective risk categories in the mix. When the stock market is flying high, the more aggressive stocks will soar and give us a positive impact far in excess of their portfolio weightings. The moderately aggressive stocks should also outpace the overall stock market. The beauty of the 60 percent, 30 percent, and 10 percent mix is that these stocks tend to zig and zag against each other, thus helping us to achieve higher and smoother returns. When it's good times in the stock market, all three segments will show strong gains. But what about other times? *Ah*, here is where the beauty of the mix truly shines. The real alpha of the stocks will appear when the stock market is more erratic, and our oasis stocks, in particular, will protect the portfolio.

The whole idea of mixing stocks that zig while others zag in your growth stock portfolio will ensure that our stocks are *rewarded* for their superior fundamentals and institutional buying pressure, which results from a high quantitative grade. Even when the stock market is weak, large funds have money they need to put to work and this will show up in the reward/risk characteristics (i.e., quantitative grade). By keeping our stocks diversified across industry groups and risk levels, and adding in some oasis stocks, we can take advantage of inefficiencies in the stock market. We saw in the late 1990s what happens when you allow market risk and an excessive bet in one kind of stock—technology stocks—to dominate your portfolio.

A lot of young fund managers believed in the technology revolution so much that they essentially overallocated in very aggressive stocks. Even funds that were once fairly stodgy and conservative were overloaded with technology names, and they never realized that all they had done was mistake beta, or returns from the market itself, for the high alpha that comes from stocks with great fundamentals and genuine institutional buying pressure.

Zigzag. Just mix in highly ranked stocks in different industries, plus some oasis stocks, combined in accordance with my recommended 60/30/10 percent mix. It's the key to consistent profits and smooth, steady growth.

Chapter Thirteen

Putting It All Together

~

*A Formula for Finding the
Best Stocks at the Best Times.*

LET'S TALK ABOUT HOW to find winning growth stocks.
We look for stocks that score high on each of the fundamental variables, are earning piles of cash, and are being
noticed by institutions. That sounds simple. However,
there is no easy way to compile the list. But, with a little elbow grease (more likely index-finger grease, as it
involves a lot of mouse clicks), it can be done. When
I first started analyzing and picking stocks back in the
1970s, access to fundamental and price data was very

restricted. It was an arduous task to dig up and enter the data. Even more restricted was access to the computing power to get the job done. I am just grateful that Wells Fargo needed free student labor and they were nice enough to let me run amuck with their mainframe!

Today, it is much easier to find the information that we need to isolate the stocks that have the variables we seek. You probably have more computing power on your laptop than we had in a room full of computers back in the day. Additionally, thanks to the Internet, you can get to the data very quickly. Federal regulations have developed over the years so that information released by corporations is available almost instantly.

Our search will begin, then, with screening for stocks that have the fundamental characteristics of great growth stocks. Screening for stocks is nothing more than electronically sorting through the universe of 5,000 or so stocks for the ones that have the fundamentals we like. There are several web sites, such as MSN, CNNMoney, and Yahoo!Finance, that have free, easy-to-use stock screeners. These web site screening programs allow you to look for lists of stocks where analysts are raising estimates, earnings have been above expectations, sales are rising rapidly, and so forth. You can search from multiple variables or just one variable at a time.

I suggest you play around with mixing and matching the variables in the screener to see what types of stocks pop up on each combination. As an example, I played around with one of the major stock-screening programs and mixed and matched a few variables. I found that by screening for sales growth over 20 percent a year, earnings growth of 20 percent a year, and an earnings surprise of over 5 percent, I produced a list of 260 stocks, many of which are in my newsletter portfolios. By screening for just stocks that had an earnings surprise in the past two quarters and at least one analyst upgrade, I came up with a very short list of 30 powerful growth stocks. Already, you can see how a little elbow grease mixing and matching just a few variables can produce a list of potential growth stock winners.

Next, starting with our list of 30, it is a very simple matter to click on any of the individual stocks to see more detailed financial information in the form of a handy company report. From sales to profit margins to future earnings estimates, you'll find data that will give you further insight into our eight key fundamental variables. In the company report, we can look to see how much cash flow the company has. It's not enough? Cross that one off and move to the next one. The report will show us whether year-over-year profit margins are expanding, and what the trend in analyst estimates has been. We can check each and every one of the variables and see if our growth stock candidate holds up to scrutiny.

Once fundamentals are checked, we move on to quantitative ratings. Where do you go to find that data? Well, if you're a mathematician you're in great shape. If not, don't panic; I promised not to leave you out there on your own, so let's take a look at the very database I use to select stocks. You'll find an incredibly user-friendly version of this database at the web site I've mentioned a few times before (www.getrichwithgrowth.com). But before you dash off to your computer to log on, let me show you how it works.

Let's say Apple (AAPL), Google (GOOG), and ExxonMobil (XOM) have made your stock list. Simply enter the ticker symbols in the user-friendly version of my database, called PortfolioGrader Pro, and up will pop a screen that looks like Figure 13.1.

As you can see, the ratings for each stock are shown in the form of letter grades—*A* (Strong Buy), *B* (Buy),

FIGURE 13.1   Ratings for AAPL, GOOG, and XOM

Portfolio Grade **B**	Total Stock Grade	Quant. Grade	Fund. Grade	Sales Growth	Operating Margin Growth	Earnings Growth	Earnings Moment.	Earnings Surprises	Analyst Earnings Revisions	Cash Flow	Return on Equity
AAPL Apple Inc. STOCK REPORT	A	A	B	B	B	A	B	A	A	C	A
GOOG Google Inc. (Cl STOCK REPORT	B	B	A	A	A	A	C	A	A	C	A
XOM Exxon Mobil Cor STOCK REPORT	B	A	B	F	B	B	C	B	B	B	A

KEY: A=Strong Buy, B=Buy, C=Hold, D=Sell, F=Strong Sell   Print Report

C (Hold), D (Sell), and F (Strong Sell). You can confirm the strength of the fundamentals for each stock, as each of our eight key variables is clearly rated. Plus, you'll see a *combined fundamental grade*, which is the *overall* fundamental grade for the stock. I'm often asked, "How can a stock be rated a C in a few variables and still get a B overall fundamental grade?" Remember, the only constant on Wall Street is *change*, and at different times different variables will be given higher weightings, because that's what's working on Wall Street at this point in time.

We still haven't addressed the real moneymaker in our overall formula—the *quantitative grade* (see Figure 13.1). This is the all-important grade of how much buying pressure is flowing into the stock. It is going to be critical for us, not just in confirming that we have good buying pressure in the stock, but in determining whether we should buy the stock at all.

Now, as promised, we're going to put the entire formula together. Knowing whether to buy or sell any given stock on Wall Street is a result of taking 30 percent of the fundamental grade and 70 percent of the quantitative grade to calculate the *total stock grade*. This is the grade that spells out, with zero guesswork, whether you should buy, sell, or hold a stock at any point in time.

Let's go back to your three stocks, Apple, Google, and Exxon. A look at Figure 13.1 will show you that, at the time we plugged in these stock symbols, Apple was a Strong Buy, while Google and Exxon were both Buys.

How do these stocks rate today? *You tell me* when you log onto my PortfolioGrader Pro tool! But don't go just yet—we still have some important ground to cover. You see, we're not done, as this chapter is called, "Putting It All Together." You now know how to find great stocks, and have clear buy/sell/hold recommendations at your fingertips. But once you find all your great growth stocks, it's equally important to know how to blend them into an optimal portfolio.

Over the years, I have put a lot of time and effort into finding the right mix of stocks to create an optimal portfolio. Because everyone's needs are not the same, and some folks may be willing to take on more risk than others, I recommend a 60/30/10 portfolio mix to begin. Specifically, I have found that having 60 percent of your portfolio in conservative stocks, 30 percent in moderately aggressive stocks, and 10 percent in aggressive stocks is an optimal mix where you can achieve steady returns without excessive risk. In my PortfolioGrader Pro tool, simply click on the Stock Report link under any graded stock, and you'll find the Risk Category clearly labeled at the top of the report. (See Figure 13.2.)

Conservative stocks have the steadiest buying pressure, so they're much less volatile than aggressive stocks;

FIGURE 13.2   Is a Stock Conservative, Moderately Aggressive, or Aggressive?

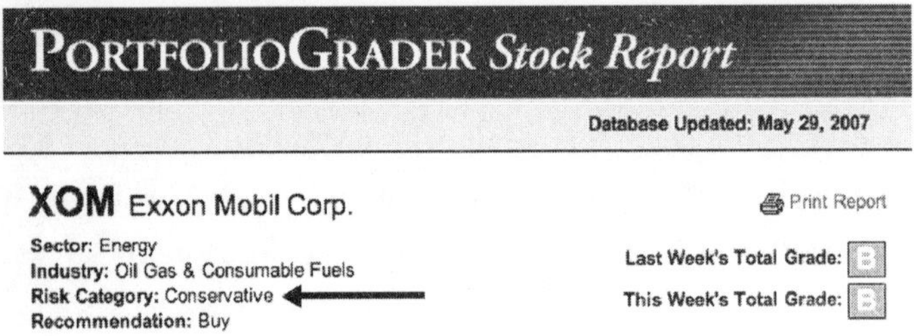

PORTFOLIO**GRADER** *Stock Report*

Database Updated: May 29, 2007

XOM Exxon Mobil Corp.   Print Report

Sector: Energy
Industry: Oil Gas & Consumable Fuels   Last Week's Total Grade: B
Risk Category: Conservative ◄────────   This Week's Total Grade: B
Recommendation: Buy

therefore, in this optimal mix, they maintain the dominant portion of the portfolio at 60 percent.

The aggressive stocks, which can be allocated to up to 10 percent of your portfolio, provide you with some exposure to the riskier stocks that can soar to ridiculous heights when the market takes off to the upside; but when the market is declining, the 60 percent in more conservative growth stocks helps offset the swings in the more aggressive positions. I also think that you should have at least 12 stocks in your portfolio that will insulate from company-specific risk. I always suggest that you put the same amount of money into each stock rather than try to fiddle with portfolio weightings on a subjective basis.

So let's say you find a total of 15 stocks and that each has a total stock grade of *A* or *B*. You would then aim to have nine conservative, four moderately aggressive, and two aggressive stocks. Keep in mind the zigzag effect I talked about earlier, and mix and match across industries and sectors that move differently from one another.

All right; now you know how to find A- and B-rated stocks and how to blend them into an optimal portfolio. The next question most investors ask me is, "Do you have any specific instructions when purchasing stocks?"

If taxes are an issue and you want to hold stocks for long-term capital gains (e.g., over 12 months), I recommend that you buy A-grade and B-grade stocks. But keep in mind you might have to hold these stocks even as they slip to a C-grade in order to achieve long-term capital gains. A-grade stocks typically remain A-rated for only four to five months, while B-grade stocks can last for an extended period of time. I manage two of my newsletters taking long-term capital gains into account, so we often own a C-stock here and there. This is fine, as a C is a Hold, not a Sell—an important distinction. Even powerful stocks sometimes have to settle down and temporarily slip to a C-grade in the midst of their impressive rallies.

I am also often asked by investors if they should use stop-losses. Given the wide swings in stock values each month, many investors think that they can lower their risk by using *stop-losses*—standing orders with your broker to sell an investment automatically if it falls to a certain price. If you are a long-term investor the answer is "no," absolutely not. For long-term investors, I'm very much against stop orders. Stop-losses are counterproductive to long-term investors as they pull you out of good stocks during momentary downdrafts and will all too often prevent you from achieving long-term capital gains.

Think of all the people who were stopped out of their stocks when the market plunged after 9/11. Those investors are probably kicking themselves today. In my long-term portfolios, I want to be as tax efficient as possible and using stop-losses makes that difficult if not impossible. A standing order like a stop-loss will execute even if you have owned the stock 11 months and 28 days, turning a potential long-term gain taxed at 15 percent into a short-term investment taxed at your top tax bracket. The best protection against market or individual stock swings is to have a diversified list of great stocks selected according to the zigzag and 60/30/10 mixes. Even if there are short-term bumps, I have found that stocks with superior fundamentals and strong buying pressure bounce back, especially when we enter earnings season.

However, if you are hooked on watching CNBC and like to trade, you could utilize a stop-loss system. I do in fact utilize stop-loss orders in one of my weekly trading services. I calculate my stop-loss points based on each stock's underlying volatility (i.e., standard deviation), which is how I set weekly stop-loss points. Please set stop-loss points carefully. If you set them too tight, then you will just end up frustrating yourself and trading excessively.

I should add that under no circumstances do I recommend utilizing a stop-loss system on thinly traded stocks; these stocks all too often move like bunnies in that they like to *sit* and then *hop,* and can be very frustrating to trade. Figure 13.3, depicting the stock performance of DXP Enterprises (DXPE), is an example of a bunny stock.

Can you imagine how frustrating this stock would be to trade? You would have to buy and hold this kind of stock to get any benefit from its underlying growth.

I should add that I do not set long-term price targets for recommended stocks. However, in all four of my newsletter and trading services, I do set near-term *buy-below* price limits, so I avoid chasing stocks when they break out and get overextended. I personally think

FIGURE 13.3   DXP Enterprises Stock Performance, June 2006–Mid-May 2007

Data Source: IDC/Exshare

that price targets based on some valuation guesstimate or point on a chart is one of the biggest snow jobs pushed on the public. Markets today consist of millions of people moving trillions of dollars around the global financial markets, and to say that we can predict exactly how this money will flow and how high it might push a stock is ridiculous. I do not think anyone can predict exactly how high a stock will go. If we have a good company with good fundamentals, then we know that the stock has a good chance to do extremely well. We should hold it, then, until the fundamentals decline or the buying pressure abates. My winning stocks have doubled, tripled, quadrupled, and even grown 10-fold or more over my years in this business. I have not found any way of knowing how high a stock will go in advance. Also, if I picked a stock and went on Bloomberg, CNBC, or Fox and set a price target 200 or 300 percent higher than it was currently trading at, everyone would think I was nuts.

When do you sell a stock? We've talked plenty about buying stocks, but it's equally important to know when to let go of a stock. Again, if you plug a stock into PortfolioGrader Pro and it's rated a *D* or *F*, *it's time to sell it*. Don't give yourself time to let your emotions kick in—just sell it and move on, because the time has come to buy a better stock.

The risk of continuing to hold shares in a *D-* or *F*-rated stock far outweighs the potential reward. Please monitor your portfolio carefully. *Don't fall in love with your stocks.* I frequently hear investors say that they don't want to sell a stock that has given them great gains over time. They want to hold it forever or do not want to pay taxes on the gain. First, the federal tax is only 15 percent under the current long-term capital gains rate. Paying a little tax on a winner before it becomes a loser is a better alternative than paying less taxes on less money. Second, stocks do not love you back. They only respond to their fundamentals and buying and selling pressures. Romantic or paternal feelings toward a stock do not play into the equation at all.

Whew! This was a very important chapter of this *Little Book.* I have explained the basic methods of our fundamental and quantitative formulas and provided you with the tools that will help you find stocks that offer the best opportunity for extraordinary growth. Investing is not necessarily easy, but it's not all that difficult, either, and should require no more than a few hours a week to search for new ideas and monitor your portfolio. There's more on monitoring to come, but now you have the basic tools to get started as a growth stock investor. Finding great stocks and mixing them into a powerful portfolio will put you on the fast track for profits and help dramatically boost your returns.

Chapter Fourteen

Quantum Leap

~

*How to Reap Spectacular Returns
from Elite "Superstocks."*

I MANAGE MY PORTFOLIO for long-term, tax-efficient gains, but some investors like to be more aggressive, less concerned with tax implications and the cost of frequent trading. As you can imagine, managing a portfolio along these lines is more time intensive, but if you are willing to deal with the increased trading and tax implications (even better, if you are trading in a tax-deferred account such as an IRA), then I have an aggressive strategy for you. This system does trade more than our regular accounts, but it is not a day-trading system by any stretch of the imagination. We have calculated that you need about a $200,000 account to trade this methodology. If you meet these parameters, this is the most powerful method of investing in stocks I have ever discovered.

Numbers and the stock market fascinate me and I spend most of my time researching these subjects, specifically looking for how to use numerical and quantitative measures to improve stock market performance. A few years ago, in our daily researching and digging my staff and I discovered something that should have been obvious but had simply never occurred to us. We discovered that stocks that scored a fundamental *A* and averaged in the top 20 percent in all fundamental categories were true superstars. This exclusive group of stocks turned over quite a bit more than our regular tax-efficient stock picks, but the returns were truly spectacular.

Furthermore, it seemed not to matter what the market did; these stocks simply appreciated in a smooth, steady manner, almost as if they were oblivious to the overall stock market. This list of stocks returned more than 50 percent per year from 1998 to 2003, a period that included the absolute worst bear market since the Great Depression. These stocks were in the top 1 percent of all stocks in my almost-5,000-stock database and they performed like the superstars they were and still are. Figure 14.1 shows the performance of what I have come

FIGURE 14.1   *Quantum Growth* **Returns versus S&P 500**

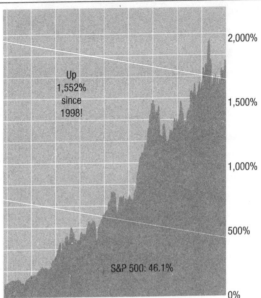

to call *quantum stocks* from 1998 to 2006. Not only is the steep rise along the way to a total return of 1,552 percent impressive; note the almost straight upslope of the line. For being "rocket-ship" stocks, they are surprisingly not as volatile as you might think.

Achieving spectacular returns with these kinds of very aggressive stocks does require more trading. In fact, if a stock drops out of the top 20 percent fundamental variables, it is immediately sold. Additionally, not only do all my quantum stocks have a *fundamental A* grade, but they must also have a *quantitative* grade of *A* or *B* to ensure that there is adequate buying pressure underneath these stocks. In other words, as soon as any quantum stock slips to a fundamental *B* grade or a quantitative *C* grade, it is immediately sold—no hesitation, no regret, just bye-bye. This makes for higher turnover, but with the super-low commission rates you can get from most brokers these days, the cost of turnover is fairly low and really doesn't inhibit performance as much as in the past.

What I especially like about the *quantum strategy* is that it takes advantage of stocks like Rochester Medical and others in their sweet spot when these stocks are benefiting from tremendous institutional buying pressure (i.e., high quantitative grades), while they have incredible sales and earnings growth. Figure 14.2 illustrates the price action when we recommended Rochester Medical and

FIGURE 14.2   Rochester Medical's Sweet Spot

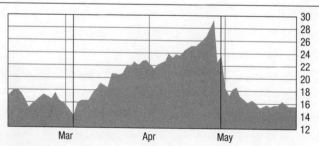

where we sold it when buying pressure abated. We locked in 51 percent gains in two months.

My list of quantum stocks are the superstars of my database. They are the equivalent of the Michael Jordans and Tiger Woodses of my intensive stock screening. These stocks are in the top 1 percent of my almost-5,000-stock database due to their superior fundamentals and institutional buying pressure, which gives them an additional boost that really kicks in the afterburners! Every quarterly earnings season I am especially excited about these stocks since I enter each earnings season locked and loaded, with nothing less than the most fundamentally superior stocks available. Buying quantum stocks creates a strong offense, which is ultimately the best defense.

Managing a portfolio of quantum stocks will be different and will involve more time and attention. Some of these stocks will be smaller stocks with less trading activity. As a result, I insist that you utilize limit orders when buying these stocks. While decimalization of stock prices has decreased the size of the bid/ask spread for many thinly traded stocks, the tighter bid/ask spread often leads to higher volatility. Since dealers aren't acting for their own accounts, the amount of stock offered has become smaller so that many thinly traded stocks are hypersensitive to trading volume. Most of the trading activity is now on the electronic crossing networks, such as Instinet.

A careless order to buy at market can often clean out the inventory of a stock for sale and cause prices to spike quickly, leaving you to pay much more for a stock than you intended.

One nice feature of the electronic marketplace is that you can set your order a little above the market price, at the most you are willing to pay. Rather than raise the offer to exploit your price, your order will be filled at the lower price. However, if you use this strategy, then I suggest you go no more than 25 cents above the current price. The one major downside of limit orders is that occasionally the stock rallies past your order point and you will not get your shares. However, if you are patient and wait several days to complete your purchase, the price will come back to you. As a result, I detest *chasing* stocks. Sometimes a stock will get away from us as these tend to be smaller and much more volatile stocks. But most of the time you will get the shares you want at the price you want and not run the price up with your order if you are patient and careful with your order placement.

I also recommend that you utilize a mental stop-loss system when trading quantum stocks. Most stock-monitoring services on MarketWatch, Yahoo!Finance, and other services can send you an alert if a stock hits your mental stop-loss point. Additionally, I should add that many of the quantum stock picks are listed on the NASDAQ market, where stop-loss orders are not accepted, anyway. Each week I calculate new stop-loss points for each quantum stock based on its respective volatility. The reason that I do not want you to place *real* stop-loss orders is because an unscrupulous specialist or trader could try to run the stock down to clean out all the stop-limit orders. The beauty of mental stops is that they are unseen by the unscrupulous. My quantum stocks are not stopped out very often, but a mental stop-loss system provides extra security, especially in the event of a sudden stock market pullback.

Utilizing stops will also raise cash quickly if the market begins a lengthier decline. Keep in mind, however, that if you can find 15 or more quantum stocks it is best to reinvest the cash in new stocks; our research shows that a diversified portfolio of all the quantum stocks frequently does very well regardless of market direction.

Earlier I said that for long-term growth stock buyers I do not like to use stop-losses, because sometimes it forces you out of good stocks at the wrong time and can interfere with achieving long-term capital gains. However, this is not what we are doing with the quantum stocks; here we employ a trading strategy where stocks will be held only when they are in the sweet spot of their fundamental cycle, combined with persistent institutional buying pressure. Use stops for these kinds of stocks. Most investors use a fixed percentage, such as 7 percent of the original purchase price, to set their stop-loss limits. However, I set my *quantum stop-loss points* based on each stock's respective weekly volatility. This way, when volatility is increasing and the stock is becoming riskier you will not be stopped out unnecessarily. Looking at the average weekly trading range for a stock will give you a much better idea of how much volatility is normal and will help you select the right price for your stop order.

This combination of power, without incurring unnecessary volatility, is what the quantum stocks are all about. Uncovering these *superstocks* has been one of the most exciting and significant events in my career. Frankly, I never cease to be amazed at how well these stocks do and at the lack of real volatility. This is the only strategy that I have found that truly does not seem to care what the market does. In 2001, 2002, and 2003, this approach did very well. The very best stocks tended to be way off the radar screen of many (but apparently known to some important players). For instance, in 2002, we ended up owning a whole bunch of small bank stocks that did very well as money left the stock market and went to banks. They were able to reinvest those into real estate loans at very profitable margins and the stocks did well. As the smaller banks got flush with cash, they were being bought by bigger banks. My quantum stock selection system picked up this economic activity and we ended up flying along very profitably, insulated from the carnage the rest of the market seemed to be experiencing.

The different types of companies that my quantum approach discovers usually surprises me. One would think that the stocks that were capable of such quantum-leap behavior would be lots of tiny technology and biotechnology stocks. Frankly, due to the strong fundamentals that I demand, we hardly ever see these kinds of stocks hit our list. In February 2007, we had investment-banking firms, specialty chemical companies, retailers, an insurance company, and even a utility on our quantum buy list—a very diversified selection among different industry groups. These are companies that are executing their business well, whatever the business is, and showing exceptional fundamental performance and attracting persistent institutional buying pressure. The best of the best and only the best will do for my quantum list.

Quantum stocks will occasionally be sold when their mental stop-loss is hit. However, if the stock remains rated a fundamental *A* grade and a quantitative *A* or *B* grade, it will often reappear after 31 days. The reason that I wait 31 days to add some quantum stocks back is that I want to avoid the *wash sale* rule, which is almost guaranteed to irritate your accountant when you buy back a stock within 30 days of having sold it. (Under the wash sale rule, your original cost basis is restored if you buy a stock within thirty days, which can be a potential nightmare when preparing your tax return.) Additionally, I want to make sure that whatever caused a stock to break down, hit its mental stop-loss limit, and fall below its normal trading range no longer persists. As long as a stock remains rated a fundamental *A* grade and a quantitative *A* or *B* grade, my research indicates it will probably bounce right back after settling down for a few weeks. When my quantum stocks get stopped out, it is usually because of sudden, fast market downdrafts. As soon as things settle down, you want get right back in there with the best of the best as the bargain hunters come out and key stocks start to rally. I recommend that you remain as fully invested as possible in the quantum stocks to achieve the smoothest, steadiest returns. When a quantum stock reaches the end of its run, my database identifies the conditions by lowering the grade, and then it will be time to sell and move on to another great opportunity.

The quantum stock list is the closest I have come to creating a "no-excuses strategy," and I love this approach to trading. Wherever the action and solid performance is, the quantum stock strategy finds it. Whether the stock market is favoring value stocks, growth stocks, small stocks, large caps, or even foreign stocks, this strategy identifies the best performance based on the strongest fundamentals, catching the sweet spot in a stock's performance cycle. If you are a very aggressive investor, comfortable with trading frequently and holding stocks for three or four months or less, then quantum stocks can be very rewarding.

Chapter Fifteen

It's the Economy, Stupid

Real Life Events Can Help Us
Find Real Profits.

IT'S THE ECONOMY, STUPID." Bill Clinton rode those four words straight into the White House back in 1992. If we change it slightly to read, "It's the economy and the market cycle, stupid," investors can ride the phrase straight to large profits by investing in the right stocks at the right time, matching their portfolio makeup to take advantage of economic events and market cycles. Investors need to be aware of the trends and cycles that can affect their portfolios, not just to protect themselves, but also to exploit them for profit.

Working the market cycle is something like going for a hike in the high mountain country. One sees beautiful vistas, undiscovered lakes, wildlife, land untouched by development. Such a journey offers great rewards. But there are dangers. One needs to be aware of weather patterns and be prepared for changes. One must be aware that wildlife is wild and that bears, mountain lions, and venomous snakes are not gentle traveling companions. Those who are not aware of the dangers that lurk in the back country are the ones who will likely need to be rescued, their travails featured on the evening news. There is little difference between the unaware hiker who gets lost in the woods and the investor who suffers grievous losses because she ignored current market conditions and dangers.

In early 2007, who didn't hear many financial talking heads and pundits profess surprise at the stock market rally? The U.S. markets, in particular, had seen almost 19 straight quarters of double-digit earnings growth, a humming economy, and strong holiday retail sales. Yes, there are problems in the subprime mortgage market, but it has to rain somewhere.

One reason that corporate earnings have been so strong is that the corporate stock buybacks have been relentless in the past three years. Further, we have experienced wave upon wave of mergers coming into the market, driving prices higher. An unprecedented amount of private equity money has been sloshing around, with investors looking to buy corporations and willing to put up significant cash. Most significantly, the private equity boom that has taken public companies private has reduced the net float of stock available. There is no letup in sight for any of these activities.

In 2006, $555.9 billion in stocks disappeared from the markets due to mergers, acquisitions, and stock buyback programs. This was the third year in a row that the amount of stock outstanding had shrunk. At the current rate of accelerating mergers, acquisitions, and stock buyback programs, $1 trillion may disappear from the U.S. stock market in 2007 alone. In fact, more than 90 percent of dealmakers (investment bankers and private equity folks) call the current merger and acquisition environment "good" or "excellent."

Those who aren't aware of where we are in the market cycle are surprised and underinvested. We, however, are always locked and loaded and go into each earnings season owning the best stocks our *quantitative* and *fundamental* models uncover. Naturally, since we have stacked the odds in our favor, we are even more confident during earnings season.

One of the more obvious trends in the market and economy is the difference in the performance cycle for stocks that fit a growth profile and for those that are considered value stocks. Value stocks have been the rage for the last several years and have outperformed traditional growth stocks. Please note that, although I am a growth stock manager, this value bias has not affected us as our fundamental and quantitative approach allows us to find the right growth stocks at the right time regardless of market conditions and bias. The reason for the value outperformance is so simple that investors and academics overlook it. Interest rates have been falling. When rates fall, the companies that are thought of as value stocks are able to refinance their balance sheets on favorable terms and improve business with the aid of cheap money. Further cheap money makes it possible for private equity funds to leverage up by buying assets and earnings as cheaply as possible. This takeover trend definitely helps the value crowd as opposed to the growth bunch.

Basically, the private equity folks are really leveraged-buyout specialists, and so they pay a lot of attention to a company's operating cash flow since they need this cash to pay off the debt they tend to borrow to acquire companies. In conjunction with the private equity boom, cash flow as a method to screen and select stocks has soared in popularity. Figure 15.1 shows how companies with strong cash flows have seen superior performance recently.

When interest rates rise, the economy tends to grow at a nice pace and consumers and businesses alike have

FIGURE 15.1   Trailing Three-Year Free Cash Flow to Market Value Performance

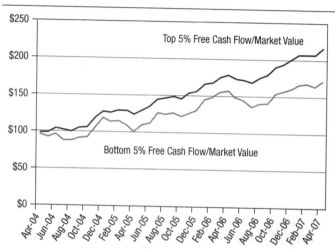

cash to spend. This cash is spent in areas that are comprised of mainly growth issues. Leisure companies, popular retailers, and new dining franchises all benefit from a growing economy. Their earnings tend to grow at a faster pace as a result of all the happy consumers coming through the doors. Technology-oriented companies also benefit, as brisk sales allow research-and-development budgets to grow, which further drives earnings at a rapid pace. This is a powerful market cycle that investors should be aware of as they allocate their money to the market. Using a combination of fundamental and quantitative screening, we put these cycles to work for us and find the companies in the industries that are hitting the sweet spot of the economic cycle.

There are other cycles at work in the marketplace that investors should know about. One strategy used by some investors (and hotly debated) is to sell in May and go away (at least until November). Those who subscribe to this method believe that you should own stocks from November 1 though the end of April and remain in cash all other times. While the evidence of this strategy has been the stimulus for much argument and dispute, the results have been powerful, as seen in Figure 15.2.

FIGURE 15.2   Sell in May and Go Away

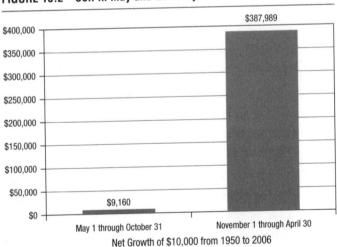

Net Growth of $10,000 from 1950 to 2006

Source: Ned Davis Research

Since 1950, this method of timing the market has been extraordinarily successful with those who practiced pretty much matching the market's rate of return by owning stocks from November to April and keeping their money in interest-bearing accounts from May to November. They earn the stock market rate of return, but are exposed to market movements only half the time. I suspect that the reason for the strength of this strategy may have something to do with individual and corporate spending habits. Companies seem to spend the bulk of their budgets early in the year on everything from maintenance to new equipment. This is often reflected in first-quarter earnings of companies that supply technology, equipment, and services to other companies and is usually reported in April. Thus, the market trends higher through the end of the quarter. Consumers, on the other hand, tend to do their heavy spending at back-to-school time and leading up through the holidays. This is reflected in the quarterly earnings released in October and January.

Also contributing to the overall trend is that investment professionals and even individual investors vacation during the summer, so that the stock market slows on declining volumes. Many of my Wall Street peers do not work in the summer. Instead, they go to the Hamptons, Nantucket, and Martha's Vineyard where they seem to "check out" during the summer months. There is also the simple fact that pensions are funded in January, and this tends to drive the market higher as well. Sell in May and go away. There are a lot of reasons it works and investors who are aware of the trends can tailor their portfolios so they are in the best stocks for the time of year.

Another market pattern that comes into play every four years is the *presidential market cycle*. As Figure 15.3 shows, the market tends to do better in the first and third years of the election cycle. The explanation for the

FIGURE 15.3   Dow Industrials Presidential Election Cycle, 1/2/1900–12/31/2006

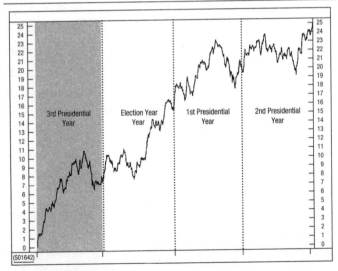

Source: Ned Davis Research

first year is simple: Investors are also voters and they tend
to be excited about the implementation of the changes
they voted into office. They are excited about the pros-
pects for the future and invest accordingly. The third
year, however, is the strongest of the cycle. The reasons
may be slightly less clear but are no less compelling. One
theory suggests that during the first two years of a presidential term, the person in office has to make tough
decisions about taxes and spending that will likely have
the most impact on the U.S. economy during the first
and second terms. However, by the third year of a presidential term, the U.S. economy is typically booming, so
the stock market explodes. The fourth year of a presidential term is not so bad, either.

I have another theory why the stock market tends to
perform so well in the third and fourth years of a presidential term. Specifically, the powerful and very biased
news media in the United States tend to back off. In fact,
immediately after the midterm elections, the supercriti-
cal news media shift gears and all of a sudden report *happy*
news. Why does this happen? The answer is *timing*.
Midterm elections take place in November and are immediately followed by major winter holidays. Who wants to
hear bad news during this time? The news media follow
their viewers and readers and provide them with what they
will buy—better news stories. During the holidays,
especially Thanksgiving and Christmas, the news media

are obsessed with reporting happy news such as the Thanksgiving parade and other feel-good stories. But how is it that happy news impacts the stock market? Well, optimism is contagious, and humans are all too often conditioned by what they watch on television and read in the papers or online.

I have one last comment on the news media. In the last couple of years of a president's term, the news media seem to back off a bit as the president increasingly becomes a lame duck. Instead, the news media turn their attention to the next potential president. It is also interesting to observe that the news media seem to be able to take on only one subject at a time, which is why we soon tire of hearing about O.J. Simpson, Anna Nicole Smith, Britney Spears, or whoever is the latest celebrity newsfest. In theory, if there were a big celebrity scandal right before an election, a hot candidate could flame out because the media would drop all their coverage.

The bottom line is this: If the folks on television are happy, consumers and investors should be happy, too. Investors who are aware of the presidential election cycle can be locked and loaded going into what has historically been the strongest period for the stock market.

There are other media cycles that have an impact on stock prices. In the summer, Congress isn't in session and political news tends to slow. To fill and sell papers and get ratings the media look for news, most of it negative, to keep people reading and watching. Investors are heavily impacted by the flow of news and this has an impact on their buying and selling patterns (yet another reason for the results of the sell-in-May strategy). As we move later into the year and begin to approach the holidays, people want happy news to reflect the season and by and large the media tend to accommodate them with more feel-good stories and happy news and the cycle repeats. Media cycles probably don't have as much of an impact as the liquidity stampede brought about by the sell-in-May crowd exiting or returning or the presidential cycle, but these cycles do have some effect. Smart investors are aware of them and use them to their advantage.

Another factor in the market and economic environments is the flow of money across asset classes. The herd-like behavior of investors, encouraged and cheered by Wall Street, often creates a rolling bubble across various assets. The most recent example is seen in the rush in and out of certain asset classes since 2000. After the stock market bubble burst in March 2000, a series of events followed that caused the stock market to falter, including the disputed November 2000 presidential election, 9/11, and the corporate accounting scandals. Between March 2000 and March 2003, when the stock market stumbled, 40 percent of all stock market investors fled. The money that left the market had to go somewhere and most of it ended up in banks, which were soon awash with new cash deposits. The bursting of the stock market bubble, with aid and comfort from the Fed cutting interest rates to all-time lows, effectively helped create the housing bubble that started unwinding in 2007. Those banks had to do something with their newfound cash and they put much of it to work as home loans.

In addition to the housing rise, we had a rise in commodity prices. Part of this was supply and demand from emerging markets, but there was also a lot of Wall Street influence on the rise. As investors soured on stocks, investment firms nonetheless needed to find something people would buy (either find a new product to sell or run the risk of ruin if you can't pay the overhead). In the wake of Eliot Spitzer's assault on big investment firms, insurance companies, and mutual fund companies, the denizens of the Street started to whisper that "Spitzer missed the commodity folks." It seems almost painfully obvious that Wall Street would turn to selling that which they thought was safe from what seemed like eternal litigation, and so they turned to commodity funds and partnerships. Since these commodity funds and partnerships paid generous up-front and trailing commissions, the amount of money that poured into these investment vehicles approximately tripled in recent years. The promoters of these commodity investments sold the public on the story of rising worldwide demand and spectacular price increase forecasts (recall what I said about buying into nice-sounding stories). And so the pool of cash rushed in to buy commodities. This bubble appears to be ending as of early 2007, prompted by the natural gas blowup in the third quarter of 2006 thanks to the Amaranth hedge fund and the fact that 2007 started with a big decline in crude oil prices. Where will the cash go now? It will probably go back to where it came from in the first place: the stock market. This bodes very well for growth stock investors.

Chapter Sixteen

It's a Small World After All

The World Is Global. Investing Should Be as Well.

Over the past several years, we have noticed an interesting occurrence in our portfolios. The *American Depositary Receipts* (ADRs) of foreign companies have begun popping up frequently in our portfolios. ADRs were specifically created to enable U.S. investors to easily buy and sell foreign stocks. There are several reasons why I like ADRs. Recent studies show foreign companies that list on U.S. exchanges are more highly valued than comparable foreign companies that don't list. Also, ADRs allow us an easy way to invest our portfolio into foreign securities, therefore tapping into these growing capital markets without the complications of currency exchange and other rules. As ADRs began appearing way too often on our buy list and too disproportionately to be mere chance, we determined that international stocks were worth investigating further. We also found that our quantitative tools worked especially well on non-U.S. stocks. In fact, our analysis worked all around the globe in both stabilized nations and fast-growing emerging markets.

As we began to delve deeper into non-U.S. issues, we found a lot of things to like about the idea of investing globally. Although the United States is one of the most innovative nations around the world, it's not the only one. New products, new ideas, and new technologies are being discovered and developed all around the world. In addition, as free trade booms, the world becomes a smaller place. A whole new world of consumer markets has opened, increasing demand for cell phones and computers, automobiles, homes, and all kinds of consumer goods and services. Banks, retailers, cement companies, and even life insurance companies have sprung up all around the planet and their burgeoning new markets of hungry consumers allow them to grow much faster than their U.S. counterparts. We also discovered, to my surprise, that 10 of the world's largest companies are located outside the United States. They may do a significant portion of their business in the United States, but home is on another shore. According to *Forbes* magazine, the largest construction, auto, business equipment, and food companies are all non-U.S. companies.

To our delight, we also found that one of the biggest hurdles to global investing for folks like us who rely on extensive examination of *quantitative* and *fundamental* data has fallen by the wayside over the last decade. Until recently, information on day-to-day non-U.S. stock prices was difficult to obtain, to say nothing of the near impossibility of accessing accurate corporate financial information. The Internet really has opened the world to almost anyone with an Internet connection, and now we can get accurate information from Hong Kong, Japan, Russia, Brazil, or any of the world's exchanges and markets with just a few clicks of a mouse. Once we had the data we could crunch it, and crunch it we did. As you can see in Figure 16.1, what we found was remarkable. As ranked by our quantitative grades, the top 10 percent of our global stock picks absolutely creamed the performance of the S&P 500. The top 5 percent doubled that return again. Clearly we were onto something that worked.

There are strong underlying reasons for the success of *global growth investing*. First, there is a sort of value

FIGURE 16.1   *Global Growth* Returns versus S&P 500

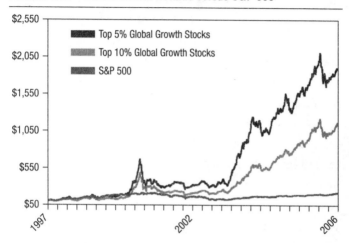

bias among most global investors, leaving growth stocks less examined and researched. As a result, when the investment community finally discovers one of these gems, it tends to rocket in price. Usually our methods have already gotten us into the stock before this happens and we get to go along for the ride. We search for global stocks using the same eight tried-and-true fundamental variables and quantitative measurements that we use on U.S. stocks and it works amazingly well, uncovering even better buying opportunities.

Part of the reason for the strong performance of non-U.S. stocks is that money has been pouring into international investments. It is not that money is necessarily flowing away from the United States; it is just flowing to other places much faster. International funds have been collecting far more dollars than U.S. funds, and the strong money flow has created buying pressure in good stocks, which gives us *alpha*, exactly what we are looking for. According to the Investment Company Institute (ICI), there is now almost as much money in international stock funds as there is in U.S.-only funds. In fact, non-U.S. funds have outsold domestic U.S. investment mutual funds by almost 4 to 1 between 2003 and 2006. The strong flows into non-U.S. markets and stocks is a relatively new phenomenon that shows little sign of abating, especially given that many non-U.S. stocks are riding a free currency tailwind from a weak U.S. dollar.

Exchange-traded funds (ETFs) are another important new development in the fund world. Traded on exchanges and offering substantial liquidity and cost advantages over traditional funds, ETFs are a fast growing source of investment cash. The international segment also dominates this area with much more cash flowing into international ETFs than U.S. indexes.

There are several reasons for this cash flow change. One of the more obvious is that investors like to diversify their holdings. Most financial advisors today suggest that their clients have some exposure to non-U.S. assets. In a smaller, more accessible world it makes sense for investors to go wherever opportunity presents itself.

Another significant reason for the money flow into non-U.S. markets and stocks is the Sarbanes-Oxley Act. Sarbanes-Oxley has led to a reduction of the number of international companies that want to list in the United States in the form of an ADR share (the media have reported extensively on the issue). With fewer ADR shares available and more money pouring into international stocks than ever before, the remaining ADR shares have soared in recent years. Ironically, Sarbanes-Oxley has effectively helped to reduce the number of ADR shares and artificially boosted the remaining ADR stocks. Sarbanes-Oxley tightened the reporting standards for companies listed in the United States and compels chief executives to sign and personally vouch for their accounting reports and releases. Many non-U.S. companies have not been interested in being this exposed to the U.S. legal system. They are well aware that the United States is the world's most litigious society and they simply have no interest in being exposed to it. As a result, many have left U.S. markets and many that might have listed their shares in the United States no longer bother. Both Hong Kong and Shanghai did more IPOs than the U.S. markets did in 2006, even though the NYSE led the world in new IPOs just five years ago, before Sarbanes-Oxley was passed. As the pool of international ADRs has shrunk in the United States, the money has followed the new names to exchanges in London, Hong Kong, and Shanghai.

Because of the recent compelling reasons to invest globally, we have made a strong push in that direction. Rather than attempt to set up accounts at exchanges and brokerages all over the world, however, I tend to favor ADRs since they are a convenient way for U.S. investors to invest in international companies—an otherwise complicated process. It is especially good to know that ADRs are traded in accordance with U.S. market regulations, so any dividend payments as well as any corporate action notification will be timely. ADRs are also convenient because they're quoted and traded in U.S. dollars on the U.S. securities markets: NYSE, AMEX, and even NASDAQ. Each ADR is backed up by a specific number or fraction of shares in the foreign company. The relationship between the number of ADRs and the number of foreign shares is often referred to as the *ADR ratio*. I find that using this way of investing allows me to avoid worries over the different regulations and currency fluctuations of the various markets around the globe.

There are close to 300 ADRs in our universe and I find that around 25 to 30 of them at any given time are strong growth opportunities. We diversify, of course, with a tendency to lean toward the larger countries and companies. We like the fact that many of these stocks are very conservative and often have large government ownership, which helps increase the feel-good and sleep-well factor of global investing. We also sprinkle money across some of the emerging markets as they can be like rocket ships when they perform well. We keep that portion small so that we can benefit nicely when they blast off but not get hurt when they fall back to earth. They are volatile, and we try to make that volatility work for us and not against us. We also make it a point to avoid countries that we see as anti-capitalist in their foreign and financial policies. Venezuela under Hugo Chavez comes to mind as a prime example of a place we will not invest because of this reason.

Why do we invest globally? Because it increases the number of opportunities available to us and because it works. The value bias of most international investors and the continuing enormous flows of cash toward non-U.S. markets combine to offer an incredible opportunity to growth investors. The information needed to analyze and invest in these markets is as available as is information on our favorite U.S. stocks. It's a whole new world out there and we think we should be a part of it and take advantage of all the growth opportunities ahead around the world. Billions of people will need new homes, roads, and infra-structures over the next 50 years. Billions of new consumers will want all the fancy goods and toys that western con-sumers have long taken for granted. There are huge new marketplaces out there, and as growth investors we can benefit as they develop.

Chapter Seventeen

A Watched Pot Will Boil

~

Unlike Water, Stocks Need to Be Carefully Watched.

"A WATCHED POT NEVER BOILS." At least that's what the old adage claims. The fact is that physics are physics and with the proper application of heat, that pot of water will boil on the 50-yard line of the Super Bowl with tens of thousands in the stands and millions watching on television. I will tell you what watching that pot can do for you: If you watch it closely, you can prevent that pot from ever boiling over. It's the same way in the stock market. By being diligent and watching your stocks closely, you can keep your portfolio boiling nicely and avoid it boiling over or evaporating. The last thing you want is for the pot to boil over or evaporate and your gains to disappear or become losses.

At my firm, we check everything on a weekly basis. In fact, we do extensive research each weekend to determine the grades for our watched stocks. We run regression tests that spit out the *reward/risk scores* that determine our *quantitative* grades and make sure we're basing our scores on the right benchmark for all the stocks in the universe. We then check the *fundamentals* based on our tried-and-true *eight variables* to gauge whether our stocks are intact and hitting on all cylinders. We do not like surprises in our office and we go out of the way to make sure the only ones we experience are positive ones. In summary, we are very diligent, hardworking folks and the fruits of our labor are updated every week.

Years ago, it was difficult for investors to keep up on all the news impacting their stocks. An investor would have to scour the pages of the daily newspapers for closing prices, important news, and earnings reports. Now, thanks to the Internet, getting the data is so easy there is no excuse for not being fully aware of all that is going on in your portfolio. Most important of all, you can manage and track your entire portfolio performance with ease and speed. The most important number you should focus on is the bottom-line performance of your entire portfolio. Day-to-day price movements in individual stocks can make you crazy, especially in high-powered growth stocks. If you are using my recommended 60/30/10 portfolio allocation and mixing in stocks that often zig when other stocks zag, the bottom line is that your overall portfolio will appreciate in a smooth, steady manner.

Regardless of what electronic or virtual tools you use to track your stocks and manage your portfolio, there is one newspaper that you should absolutely be reading. It is *Investor's Business Daily®* (*IBD*). This newspaper will educate and inform you about the most important market events and will make you a better investor than any business school ever could. *IBD* is laid out in an easy-to-read format, so all the important news "jumps out" at you. The combination of *IBD* and my database tools will give you a one–two punch that can seriously supercharge your investments.

Now pop over to www.getrichwithgrowth.com. You look at each stock in your portfolio and get the quantitative and fundamental scores for each stock using my stock-rating database. As you can see in Figure 17.1, you'll find the ratings in a simple letter-grade format with an *A*-grade being the best grade for each category and an *F*-grade being the worst. This makes it very quick and easy to check your stocks each week and make sure you

FIGURE 17.1   Stock Ratings in PortfolioGrader Pro

Portfolio Grade A	Total Stock Grade	Quant. Grade	Fund. Grade	Sales Growth	Operating Margin Growth	Earnings Growth	Earnings Moment.	Earnings Surprises	Analyst Earnings Revisions	Cash Flow	Return on Equity
▼▲	▼▲	▼▲	▼▲	▼▲	▼▲	▼▲	▼▲	▼▲	▼▲	▼▲	▼▲
AAPL Apple Inc. STOCK REPORT	A	A	B	B	B	A	B	A	A	C	A

don't end up being surprised when the risk level rises in a stock and the inevitable price deterioration begins.

We have examined different cycles in the market and in the economy that may impact how stocks do overall. Building a portfolio of stocks with the help of my stock-rating database in the manner suggested does give a lot of protection from market moves, but it is impossible to negate all of the impact. For example, if you have large long-term profits in a particular stock and it's the last few weeks of April, you might want to consider selling some shares knowing that the *sell-in-May-and-go-away* crowd will be putting pressure on overall stock prices the following month. If it is late October and you have cash on hand, you might want to go ahead and get it invested, knowing that the guys who sold in May will be back soon looking to get money into stocks as quickly as possible.

Let me give you an example of how I look at things when investing. Going into mid-2007, as I looked at the landscape of the stock market I knew that value stocks had outperformed growth stocks for over seven years, which is an unprecedented run. I know that the sell-in-May crowd will soon sell off, and that most pensions and IRA accounts were funded between November and April 15. It's also the third year of a presidential term, which will have me becoming very bullish, since this has historically been a strong year for the stock market. All of these factors combine to make me feel very bullish on stock prices and so I'll want to be as fully invested as possible.

Always check your mix. Try to stay with my recommended 60/30/10 allocation as much as possible. If the market is awash in liquidity, that 10 percent in aggressive stocks can rocket upward, and if you are not careful you will find yourself overinvested in superaggressive and riskier stocks as the market peaks. As the market turns down, this will not be a fun position. If you are fairly conservative in your approach to growth stock investing, make sure you have as many A-rated stocks as possible and watch them for grade changes. Likewise, if we are in a difficult market such as 2002, the aggressive stocks may well fall in price while the more conservative ones rise, and you need to get some money to work in the aggressive names as they are now an enormous bargain. Even though I do not generally time the market, I find that rebalancing my 60/30/10 allocation keeps me buying the right type of stocks at the right time, becoming more conservative as prices rise and aggressive as they fall. That runs counterintuitive to the way most of us think, so once again relying on the numbers overcomes fear and greed and keeps us on the right path.

Obviously, when you sell a stock it will be time to go find another one. In addition to replenishing your portfolio, you should run a new search of all stocks once every month to every three months. At a minimum, I search for new opportunities every March, June, September, and December, because these times are the last months of the reporting quarters for most U.S. companies and in the subsequent months they will begin to report their earnings to investors. These times mark earnings season and I want to enter them fully locked and loaded with only the very best stocks in my account. I run my searches and compare any new stocks I may find against the ones I own. If I find a couple of new stocks that have outstanding fundamental variables and great quantitative scores, I want to add those stocks to my portfolio going into earnings season. As I look through the stocks I already own and find one that is okay in five or six variables and has slipped from an *A* rating to a *B*, I am probably going to sell that stock and replace it with my new discovery. The original stock may still be a good stock, but I will have found an even greater stock to replace it and I am determined to be locked and loaded with only the *very best* stocks in my portfolio for the upcoming earnings season.

Think of it this way. You are a baseball coach going into the season and you have an okay second baseman who can still hit about .250 and has a decent glove; he will do okay in that spot and probably won't hurt you. But now he's a little older, his legs will be a little slower and his batting average *has* dropped a tad. You can make do with him. He is a nice guy and has been on the team for a while and you would probably be sad to see him go. But, you find that you can replace him with a 20-year-old phenomenon who hits .350, will probably have 30 home runs, runs like the wind, and plays the infield like a Hoover vacuum. Guess what? You are going to have a new second baseman this year.

Never fall in love with your second baseman or your stocks. I have been known to fire people who fall in love with stocks and who are slow to sell. In order to win, you have to be willing to make the changes and add the new, more powerful stocks to your account. Focusing on the numbers and remaining unemotional about our stocks is even more important as we approach earnings season. This is when all the good stuff can happen. *Earnings surprises*, *accelerating earnings momentum*, *positive analyst earnings revisions*, and so on—all of these happen on a regular basis during earnings season. The companies we select have the potential at any time for huge upside earnings reports and surprises, and we have already discussed how these occurrences can send stocks on a long, smooth upward run. To put it simply, each quarterly earnings season is the equivalent of Judgment Day for each and every stock.

Above all, keep learning. I continually study the market, searching for what works and new ways to apply my principles to growth stock investing. This is why something as simple as reading *Investor's Business Daily*® is so important. It is impossible to know everything there is to know about this game, but always be looking, studying, and evaluating anything that might influence your investments. I think you have to always be learning and testing new things and new ideas. Anytime I meet somebody who is real cocky and thinks he knows everything there is to know about the stock market, I know that he has probably found one variable that worked for a short period of time and he is on the verge of learning a very painful lesson. The stock market can deal out humility better than anything else I have ever found. Just when you think you are smart, the market will show you just how dumb you are.

Keep an eye on the boiling pot that is your stock portfolio at all times. Fortunately, thanks to modern technology, monitoring your stock portfolio has never been easier. Be aware of the changes in your portfolio and where we are in the market and economic cycle. Always be searching for new and better stocks to replace the ones you own. The objective is to find the best stocks on a fundamental and quantitative basis, stocks that are heating up from persistent institutional buying pressure, and then stay with these stocks while they bubble along without overheating and spilling out all our profits.

Chapter Eighteen

Lions and Tigers and Bears, Oh My!

Beware of These Dangers on Wall Street.

JUST AS DOROTHY and her intrepid companions were worried about what they might face in the forest, investors need to be aware of the ways they can be deceived or tricked when investing in the stock market. Most of the time, relying on the *eight fundamental variables* that I have outlined for you is going to keep you out of trouble—but not all of the time. There are many ways that companies and unscrupulous promoters have come up with over the years to deceive and defraud you and I want to take some time to warn you what to be on the lookout for.

One of the worst forms of deception can come from the companies themselves. *Accounting fraud* has been around as long as individuals have traded stock in the underlying corporation. We have seen over the past several years some of the more unscrupulous examples meet their just reward in companies like Global Crossing, Enron, and WorldCom. However, while these companies and their managements were punished, many investors lost billions of dollars. Although a lot of loopholes have been closed, executives who want to mislead investors to think things are rosier than they actually are will find new ways to deceive. For years, I have opposed such trickery and pointed out the problems with pooled-interest accounting and stock options that were not expensed. Pooling-of-interest accounting is an extremely misleading accounting gimmick, and I am proud to say that I have spoken out against it loud and often.

This method was used primarily in mergers and acquisitions. It provided a way for companies to dress up their financial reports so that losses and poor earnings were hidden from investors. Before the demise of pooling-of-interest accounting, all a company had to do was to acquire another company and then book its revenues and defer and reamortize its expenses. This was effectively "smoke-and-mirrors accounting," since the more companies that a company acquired, the more it could effectively manipulate its books. Not only were companies trying to hide a bad quarter via pooling-of-interest accounting, but some, like WorldCom, were manufacturing their alleged growth via acquisitions.

Just before WorldCom blew up, it was trying to buy Sprint. Had it actually bought Sprint, WorldCom would have been able to book virtually all its revenues while deferring much of its expenses, and continue its fraud. How Citigroup analyst Jack Grumman could not have seen through WorldCom's fraud was a bit perplexing, except that he also had an immense underwriting conflict due to the fact that Citigroup was one of WorldCom's lead underwriters. I must admit that WorldCom's fraud was extremely complex. It is one of the few companies that I can remember that distorted its cash flow and paid more taxes than it had to in order to hide and perpetuate its accounting fraud.

The best way to protect yourself from fraud when screening stocks is to make sure that a company's operating margins, return on equity, and cash flow receive high grades. I have never seen any company successfully manipulate more than two of these three variables.

Thankfully, in 1999, the Federal Accounting Standards Board (FASB) finally did away with pooling-of-interest accounting and forced companies to use the purchase method, which shows the combined company as it really is. FASB also addressed the matter of stock options, and in 2004 passed Statement No. 123, which forced companies to show stock options as an expense instead of hiding the dilutive effect that exercising these in-the-money employee options actually caused. These were all solid steps forward, but deceptive practices still exist and others we haven't thought of will appear in the future.

One of the management practices that I consider among the worst is managing earnings. Public companies report earnings according to *generally accepted accounting principles* (GAAP), but even these guidelines leave room for accountants to make the numbers fit the picture they wish to draw. The intense quarterly focus by the investment community on quarterly earnings reports puts pressure on management to hit or exceed its numbers every three months. Rather than report a bad number that would drive the stock lower, management may massage its numbers to meet Wall Street expectations. The two ways companies can manage earnings is by the use of one-time charges and investment gains. By writing off items such as ongoing construction costs as a one-time expense that is not relevant to the current situation, they are able to hide cost overruns or investments that did not work out well. GAAP is supposed to prevent earnings management, but it is not unusual to see some companies take "one-time charges" pretty much every quarter to mask their losses and mistakes.

Investment income, tax refunds, and other extraordinary items that are reported as regular earnings can also be employed to blur the true picture. Reporting income from an investment can easily disguise the fact that the core day-to-day business is suffering. If the company is unable to repeatedly show investment gains (and it surely will be, as it will eventually run out of cash to invest when the core business is hemorrhaging money and consumes investable dollars), the true earnings will be seen and its stock will go down in the process. If you set up your portfolio in the manner I recommend through one of the programs available on a financial web site such as Yahoo! Finance, you can receive alerts that will notify you when one of your stocks reports earnings. Be very wary of companies that seem to book extraordinary items as part of their normal operating earnings!

Slush fund accounting is another device used to hide the true picture. Here, the company holds back and doesn't report all of a good quarter's earnings and, instead, saves them to show in a later quarter that has poorer performance. On the face of things, this wouldn't seem to be such an egregious practice. However, quarterly performance is quarterly performance, and you don't want to be holding the stock of a company that is experiencing declining earnings but is hiding this fact by managing its earnings. The books should be the books and management should be focused on managing the business, not getting illusory good results by managing its books. A variation of this practice is sometimes used by banks. Banks lend money they receive as deposits. It is a fact of life that some of these loans will go bad, so banks have to maintain a reserve to protect themselves from bad loans. There are regulatory guidelines on minimum reserve levels, but ultimately a bank will set its own level. It is a relatively simple matter to make some sickly loans seem miraculously healthy when earnings are less than management or investment analysts want them to be: Just take the money out of reserves and declare it a profit. Be wary of banks that lower reserves one quarter, as they may well be managing earnings to make themselves look healthier than they really are.

Backdating stock options has become another problem for companies and investors. Employee stock options are granted to top executives as additional rewards and as a way to get around salary cap restrictions. The practice of granting stock options exploded after the Clinton Administration passed a bill that effectively limited executive compensation to $1 million per year, since any salary above that threshold could not be deducted from a company's tax return. As a result, in some years an executive would make $1 million while in other years that same executive would make $600 million ($1 million in salary and $599 million in stock options). Disney's former chairman, Michael Eisner, was probably the most famous CEO for receiving extraordinary compensation some years from big stock option grants.

In theory, giving executives an additional incentive to perform well is sound: The higher the stock price goes, the more valuable their options become. However, the practice has mutated from a performance incentive into a way to mask executive pay. Companies have been backdating option grants to a date when the stock price was much lower than it is today, making the options far more valuable to executives. There are literally dozens of investigations going on into major companies that hid executive pay in this manner. It is not illegal to compensate executives with stock options, provided the terms have been clearly disclosed to shareholders and properly accounted for in income statements and tax returns. In most cases, however, they were not reported and ended up being hidden compensation costs that inflated earnings higher than they actually were.

One of the greatest dangers to investors is Wall Street hype. It is important to remember that Wall Street is essentially a sales machine. Investment businesses exist to sell us investment products from stocks and bonds to mutual funds and other fancier offerings. Although the ads for the firms make them seem like kindly rich uncles who just want to help you, you have to keep in mind that what these firms really want is to sell you stuff. I think that most brokers and financial advisors truly do want you to do well and prosper, but keep in mind that their first priority is to see themselves do well—by selling more of what they have.

It is so easy to get caught up in the hype. From financial news shows to Internet sites, magazines, and newspapers, a barrage of messages come at us every day, all day. The talking heads from the money management and brokerage firms who go on the air or who are quoted in the press with confident forecasts for their favorite stocks or great gains ahead for their funds are trying to get you to buy stuff. These people, good, bad, or indifferent, are not your kindly old uncle or aunt. They are salespeople. When they do a public offering for a company, they want you to buy the shares, so of course they will tell you that the stock that they just underwrote is a great company.

The underwriters and brokerages need your buying action to make their salaries and earnings and future business happen. The more they sell, the better they look to their corporate clients and the more business and fees they will get the next time they need to raise money.

Since companies are not going public as fast as they used to, the investment bankers on Wall Street are now changing the way that they generate their fees. The boom in private equity has been so strong that from 2004 through 2006 the amount of stock available was reduced. Private equity funds have bought out a lot of listed companies and taken these shares out of the marketplace. In fact, in 2006, $555.9 billion in stocks disappeared due to all the mergers, acquisitions, and stock buyback programs.

The reason that you see that these private equity folks will step in to a pay a premium for many publicly traded companies is because they have concluded that they can strip out key assets for extra dividends or reorganize the company to further boost its return on equity (ROE). Companies with a high ROE are typically the most likely to be acquired by the private equity firms.

Another example of recent hype has been the boom in commodity partnerships I mentioned earlier. I am convinced that the commodity boom was partly the result of Wall Street pushing commodity funds since they weren't generating much new business in stocks. When a sector is hot, you can be sure the big firms will create a fund that specializes in that area—not because it is good for your financial future but because it is easy to sell. I have been around this business a long time and I have seen the cycle over and over again. We saw real estate funds in the early 1980s, Internet funds in the 1990s, and in the early 2000s, we got commodity funds. Whatever is easy to sell, Wall Street is going to sell you.

In addition to suffering the inevitable downturn that would naturally befall them, many commodity funds stumbled after Amaranth, the multi-billion-dollar hedge fund specializing in energy, imploded due to some natural gas contracts that were "off the books" that then appeared "on the books" and sent natural gas futures plummeting. The resulting implosion hurt many commodity funds (run by managers who no doubt wondered how Amaranth got so dominant in natural gas trading and was able to have natural gas contracts off the books that they could not see). Whether these off-the-books natural gas contracts were legal is another matter, but one thing is certain: Amaranth was out of bounds and its portfolio was not as transparent as it should have been.

In addition to corporate fraud, management massaging the books, and Wall Street hype, there are also very real scams and frauds perpetrated by unscrupulous operators who engage in pump-and-dump schemes. The practice has been around forever and will be around forever as long as conmen can get unwary investors excited about a penny stock they purport will be the next Apple Computer or Microsoft. Back in the day, we'd regularly get their phone calls and direct-mail solicitations. Now these folks use fax machines and e-mails to pump up thinly traded, illiquid stocks. Using the vital fundamental and quantitative methods that I have taught you in this book will protect you from mundane promotions and sublime operators.

Finally, I have recently seen a new game that has me a little concerned as it may become yet another source, along with stock promotion and short covering, of potentially distorting the alpha component in my quantitative analysis. This is something I call the *ETF effect*. ETFs are among the hottest products on the Street right now, popping up like daisies, and their potential impact is enormous, particularly in the effect they can have on stock prices as they rebalance. Because most of these funds are new, most of the rebalancing is due to buying action. As a result, stocks get bid up because the ETFs need new shares, not because they are performing well. The demand is so strong that many ETFs are borrowing stocks from large firms and banks. In fact, Bank of America has found this to be such a lucrative business that it is offering free trading accounts with no commissions just to get its hands on shares that it can then lend to new funds at a fee. Since I rely on fundamentals and buying pressure, stocks that are going up on ETF buying should not appear on my lists. That said, you should be mindful of the potential impact these new investment funds can have on stocks.

Using the combination of fundamentals and quantitative factors to buy growth stocks in the manner outlined in this book should keep you out of harm's way. Stocks with manipulated earnings will probably fall short on our cash flow screens and be eliminated from consideration. Stocks that are pure hype jobs may show signs of positive reward/risk but will otherwise fail across most of our fundamental variables and never hit your radar screen. My most important investment strategy may well be to keep my emotions out of the process and just stick with the numbers. If we are unemotional in our approach it is hard for the Wall Street sales machine or dishonest accountants or unscrupulous operators to suck us into the cycle of fear and greed on which they depend.

Chapter Nineteen

Keep Your Eyes on the Prize

———— ❧ ————

Why the Glass Is Always Half Full.

IN MY OPINION, to be a growth stock investor you ultimately have to be an optimist. There are always going to be bumps in the road when you invest in the stock market. Even when you invest in only the very best stocks and control your risk, you will still hit a bump or two. You will hit fewer bumps than many others who aren't so rigorous, but hitting a bump or two is part of the landscape. I try to avoid the pain by making sure that I own the very best stocks for the environment, but I know there will still be some down days.

I stay focused on the fact that, over the long run, investing in stocks has been proven to be the best means to get rich in the markets. Stocks have outperformed bonds and bills and beat inflation over the long run, and I believe that they always will. Numerous studies from such academic luminaries as Roger Ibbotson, as well as Dimson, Marsh, and Staunton in their great book, *The Triumph of the Optimists*, have proven the point time and time gain. Bumps aside, the place to be to build wealth is the stock market. As I have said several times, I am a numbers guy, and the numbers say that stocks are where the money is. In the grand tradition of Willie Sutton, I am going to be where the money is!

This is a good time to review the *quantitative rating system* we use that identifies the *buying pressure* underneath each stock so we can see which stocks are attracting institutional buying pressure. The *fundamental rating system* we use grades stocks on tried-and-true fundamental factors. The stocks with the highest fundamental ratings also tend to attract institutional buying pressure, especially during each quarterly earnings season. So, it is hard for me to be pessimistic when I can stack my portfolio with favorable odds. And you can stack the odds in your favor, too, and become a growth stock optimist. It is very exciting to enter earnings season each quarter locked and loaded with fundamentally superior stocks! How can you not be optimistic?

If you want to be a pessimist, there are lots of things around to worry about. Right now, in 2007, you can worry about the Iraq situation, North Korean nukes, inflation, deflation, a dysfunctional Congress, global warming, and even Britney's bad behavior. In the 1990s, many worried about botched healthcare reform, Middle-East tensions, Y2K, O.J. Simpson, and plenty of other news that made for sleepless nights. In the 1980s, we worried about the Cold War, junk bonds, the AIDS epidemic, and Exxon Valdez. That was all good stuff to worry about. We can look at every decade and find much to give us concern and fret over—and we can say that any or all of these things are reasons not to invest in the stock market. The fact is that there will almost always be a crisis of some kind—but nearly every concern has been resolved or abated. Society has mostly marched forward with more innovation, productivity, and profits than ever before. History suggests that optimism is not unfounded. Humans have a long track record of solving their problems and improving their situation.

Let's say that you believe that optimism in the market is the way to go, but that a nagging voice deep inside gives you pause for concern. Turn to *oasis stocks* that will *capitalize* on the problems in the world. Are you worried about the Middle East's endless conflict? Look for our highly graded defense stocks (e.g., Lockheed Martin, Raytheon, and Rockwell Collins). Let's say that you are worried about reduced oil availability and increased energy costs; then check out which energy companies rank the highest and seem to profit from chaos. Do you worry about global warming? Screen for companies that might profit from stricter environmental controls. Let's look at a little example: During hurricane season you might want to profit from increased trading in weather contracts; just key in the Chicago Mercantile Exchange (CME) and the Intercontinental Exchange (ICE) to see how they rank in our database. With the right tools and analysis, even a half-empty glass will soon get fuller. The world around you may be full of danger, but you can create a portfolio that rises above it.

Additionally, whenever there has been a crisis in the world, it has all too often been an incredible buying opportunity. Check out Figure 19.1, which shows the market's upward march in spite of the various crises that have occurred.

So if it's possible to profit even in the face of doom, why is there so much bad news circling around us? Let's face it: Bad news sells books and newspapers; it sells ads on TV and collects clicks on the Internet. Doom-and-gloom

FIGURE 19.1   S&P 500, 1925–July 2006

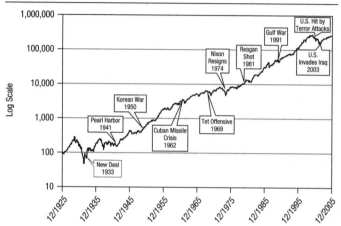

Source: Ned Davis Research

gurus seem to always make the bestseller lists with titles that tell us *Why the World Will Collapse in the 1970s*, *Why the World Will Collapse in the 1980s*, and *This Time I Really Mean It: It's All Going to Collapse This Decade*. Bad news feeds on our fears and it works as a selling tool. A look at the headlines on CNN's web site on any given day shows lots of things to worry about. But I'm an optimist. Let's take a look at the rest of the site and see what else is going on. In the health section, cancer death rates have fallen again and the Alzheimer's gene has been discovered, inching us toward finding a potential cure. In the technology section, we find that Netflix has started delivering movies over the Internet, maximizing our leisure time; an airliner has been fitted with an antimissile system, making air travel even safer; and the use of solar power is growing and lowering energy costs. The fact is that there are a lot of good and great things going on around us every day that point to a very bright future.

I don't know what the next breakthrough industry or discovery will be. I do know that when I look at the future and the possibilities I find it exciting, both personally and professionally as a growth stock investor. Nanotechnology is proceeding further every day and the health issues alone with this exciting research are staggering. Alternative energy research is picking up steam, possibly leading us toward lower energy costs (which implies higher profits). Medical science is working away at curing diseases and lengthening our life span. Technology is constantly improving our productivity and making our lives easier. Think about it: Just 10 years ago, the idea of iPods, hybrid cars, and gene therapy seemed a little science-fictionish. It is impossible to predict which ideas will advance and which breakthroughs will change and improve our lives, but innovation and discovery will happen.

In addition to enjoying innovation personally, I am also optimistic because I can enjoy new discoveries professionally by being invested in the very best stocks that will improve our future. When someone does produce a medical breakthrough that cures Alzheimer's or cancer, or an energy company finds an alternative to oil that lowers our costs, my focus on fast-growing companies with sound fundamentals will recognize them and I will own the stocks of these companies that will produce powerhouse sales and earnings. Being optimistic enough to plan for the positive outcomes that the future will bring us will make us rich— so that we can personally enjoy the benefits of innovation.

The types of companies I own are the ones that will produce breakthroughs and profits. My focus on strong fundamentals ensures that if a company has a new product or service that will be in high demand and generate fast-growing sales and profits, it will show up in our portfolios. These companies tend to dominate their space in the market and generate strong cash flows for research and development, making new discoveries possible. Just a quick look at our buy list in early 2007 shows companies involved in and leading the way in a variety of exciting fields. Angeion is a leader in noninvasive heart and lung diagnosis and treatment systems. NutriSystem is leading the way in healthy scientific approaches to weight loss. DirecTV has changed the world of home entertainment. Gilead is engaged in gene research with the potential to produce blockbuster lifesaving drugs and treatments. Growth companies tend to be innovative companies that are willing to take business risks to discover new products that can change the landscape in health, in science, and even in leisure goods and services. When new discoveries are made and new companies step forward, we will own them in our portfolios. These firms can't have outsized success and leadership and not show up on our radar screen. I might not have been able to predict the success and market dominance of Apple Computer's iPod, but my models could and did.

I also find it a lot easier to be an optimist by owning a diversified portfolio of these types of exciting stocks. Not only do I keep the portfolios spread across different industries, but I follow my 60/30/10 mix at all times. This gives me the right mix of industries across all types of stocks. I know that in a bumpy market my *conservative* stocks will tend to protect my portfolio from severe declines, while in a fast-rising market my *moderately aggressive* and *aggressive* stocks will give me all the zing I need to rise even faster. This mix has worked extraordinarily well over the years in keeping us fully invested and allowing us to withstand all the bumps the market and economy can throw at us.

There's another reason I'm an optimist. Growth investing works. It's battle tested. I originally discovered the strong performance of high-alpha stocks back in the 1970s, while a student. Since then, we have been through hyperinflation, the Cold War, the Crash of 1987, two wars in Iraq, the Internet meltdown of 2000, and guess what? It still works. Because I am a self-confessed geek I am always studying the markets and exploring new ideas to augment my models. We have carefully and completely tested a variety of fundamental variables to find those that work best, and those are the ones that form the basis for selecting the stocks that go into our portfolios. High-alpha stocks that are moving up because of strong buying pressure from mutual funds and hedge funds have given us an edge on the market that has lasted over 30 years. It is easy to be an optimist when you know that you have powerful tools and techniques for selecting wonderful growth stocks that will lead the way in a market advance.

FIGURE 19.2   Performance of _A_-Rated Stocks

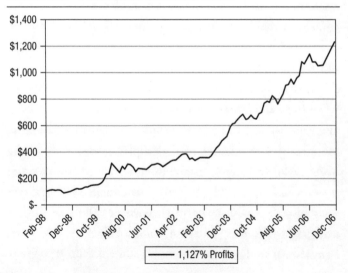

One picture is worth a thousand words. Figure 19.2 shows the results of our top-rated stocks. Since 1998, to say that the market has been turbulent is an understatement. We experienced the dot-com bubble bursting, a contested presidential election, the impeachment debate of a sitting president, and, tragically, the horrors of 9–11 and the wars in Afghanistan and Iraq that followed. Through it all, the *A* stocks, that optimistic group of overachievers, not only outperformed the market, they trounced it. There were bumps along the way, as the chart clearly shows, but the list of *A* stocks averaged better than 30 percent a year though all the trials and tribulations of the past eight years. When the market resumed its climb in 2003, these stocks turned from outperformers to afterburners. Having these types of tools available to me makes me an optimist and I will remain one throughout my investing career.

Let the naysayers and doom-and-gloom merchants sell newspaper and Internet ads. I will place faith, as all growth stock investors do, in humankind's fundamental desire to make our world a better place, safer for ourselves and our loved ones, and more enjoyable and more productive and profitable. It is these motivations that will produce the new technologies and discoveries that will lead to new growth companies with stocks that offer high returns to investors. It has been that way pretty much since the dawn of time and certainly the dawn of the markets over 100 years ago, when innovation accelerated. With all the research going on today, and all the incredible breakthroughs and discoveries of just the last 10 years, how can one not be an optimist and be almost in awe of the wonderful things to come?

And so, dear investor, my wish for you is simple. I want you to begin your investing journey with a renewed sense of optimism. The proven market-beating formula and other key lessons we've talked about in this *Little Book* are yours for the profit-taking. Begin using them today, and for many more years to come, and no matter what the market has in store, you can reap the kind of returns that can fulfill your financial dreams.

Of course our journey isn't over with the last page of this book. Remember, I'm arming you with my exclusive stock-rating tool (www.getrichwithgrowth.com), so you can take what you've learned cover to cover and apply it in today's investing world, *instantly*.

I'll see you online.